ethereum

preview

D0121845

blockchains, digital assets, smart contracts,
decentralized autonomous organizations

Henning Diedrich

Wildfire ★ Publishing

The information provided in this book is strictly for educational purposes. Although considerable effort has been made to ensure that the information was correct at time of writing, there are no representations or warranties, express or implied, about the completeness, accuracy, reliability, suitability or availability with respect to the information, products, services, or related graphics contained in this book for any purpose. Any use of this information is at your own risk. The author does not assume and hereby disclaims any liability to any party for any loss, damage, or disruption caused by errors or omissions, whether such errors or omissions result from accident, negligence, or any other cause. The information described within this book are the author's personal thoughts. It is not intended to be a definitive set of instructions for any project. There may be other technologies or materials not covered. It is recommended that you consult a technologist for the needs of your particular project.

Blockchains are seeing a lot of ongoing development. You might benefit from using the most up to date version of this book. This edition is from late 2016.

0.9.7.1

preview 3

**Please send feedback to
ethereum.book@gmail.com**

für Pit

Blockchain for the Non-Technical

This book aims to help you get your head around blockchains in general and around Ethereum specifically.

As Ethereum is currently the pre-eminent blockchain, it makes sense as a reference point. The essential stuff is roughly the same for any blockchain.

As IBM's official liaison to the Ethereum core developers I frequently gave talks on blockchain topics around the world. After one keynote I was asked for a non-technical guide to understand blockchains. This is it.

It is written for people with a fast grasp, who are not programmers. Reading this should give you the basics to cut through the hype and to identify blockchain opportunities in your professional domain.

There are tiny bits of code, which can be admired and skipped.

We'll look at Ethereum's benefits first, how it is used and what can be done with it, then explain blockchain machinery, visiting the terms that you'll be confronted with in every discussion about its application. Exactly what you need to tell the signal from the noise in the echo chamber of honest misunderstandings and desperate marketing.

We take a good hard look at limitations, throw in some history and names and give a realistic outlook.

The index reads like an FAQ[1] and you can use the book like that. However, there is a strong build up, one chapter leading to the next, as an optimized path to understanding all the interconnected, moving parts. There's quite a number of them.

Blockchains are not a trivial topic. Getting it takes a moment. Maybe don't be shy to re-read.

The fact that blockchain client programs are small has fooled many people into believing it can't possibly be that hard. However, the challenges are in the implications.

---

1 'Frequently asked questions' – a list of expected questions often found in software documentation.

Doors Just Opened,
Pick Your Seat

What's in this book will put you far ahead of almost everyone outside the core bubble.

If you find something explained badly, please yell at me at: ethereum.book@gmail.com.

A deep dive into this field now – at least getting started – will help you to become part of the fun ahead. It should allow you to stand out, land deals or a great job. Or change the world.

It will also make you see first hand how early we are in the game. Take your time! It's worth it.

Hopefully, we will find a contributor to the blockchain community in you, strengthening the portfolio of real-world use cases.

Ideally, you'll learn to navigate your own uncharted course through your domain and revolutionize it, applying blockchain tech where – you know – it really makes sense.

Index

Disclaimer

Opinions in this book are mine, not those of IBM.

I am not an Ethereum spokesperson either.

Feedback

Please use ethereum.book@gmail.com for feedback or questions. I'll be happy to hear what you felt was missing or presented out of order, no matter your background.

My twitter handle is @hdiedrich. It's where I announce where I talk and where the slide decks and videos end up afterwards.

Blue Horizon

If you want to see the blockchain in action and like trying something new with your Raspberry Pi,[2] please check out the IBM Blue Horizon project for *decentralized, autonomous edge computing* at *http://bluehorizon.network*.

We made an effort to make it easy for you to join our test network. You can even create your own decentralized, Raspberry Pi–based apps. Blue Horizon is one of the first platforms to actually use blockchain technology rather than being a plan or an experiment.

It lets you track satellites and planes, pool weather data or inspect radio frequencies listened to by a peer's Raspberry Pi, anywhere in the world.

---

2   A minimal computer, 2 x 3.5 x 1 inch

Credits

Thanks to Vitalik for all the magic swords & ponies.

Thanks for making this a better book to Martin Becze, Pindar Wong, Vitalik Buterin, Bettina Warburg, Scott Devine, Harald Stieber, Marco Heinrich, Holger Kache, Heinrich Dröge, Aeron Buchanan, Christopher Dye, Gordon Friebe, Adam Kocoloski, Mac Devine, T.J. Saw, Joachim Lohkamp, Carolyn Rickert, Joseph Chaw, Arkadiy Paronyan and Tim Swanson.

Thanks for spotting all the typos to Bettina and Vitalik.

Special thanks for language support to Alice.

Props to the Open Office and GIMP teams.

THE WORLD COMPUTER

"Ethereum is a community-driven project aiming to decentralize the internet and return it to its democratic roots.

"It is a platform for building and deploying applications which do not need to rely on trust and cannot be controlled by any central authority."

Ethereum Foundation

Reality Check

Nobody needs It.

On a panel discussion I moderated, Sarah Meiklejohn of the University College London, dryly observed that, so far, no one coming to her for advice about blockchains turned out to actually have any need for it in the first place.

Let that sink in. No one. It's all hype.

Well, except it's not.

Blockchains will change commerce.

Just like highways and the Internet itself, they will bring about pervasive change through a simple, basic function.

Blockchains collapse agreement and execution.

Because a *smart contract* both *is* the agreement and *executes* it. In business, governance and law.

They are 'collapsed' into one thing, not just simplified or packaged together.

"Magically," the code you write to define an agreement will eventually send funds left or right, as expressed in the source code of the contract.

Currently, Ethereum is by far the most advanced and robust blockchain available. The competition is arriving. Bitcoin is holding its ground. But today, for all intents and purposes beyond cryptocurrency, Ethereum is *the* block-chain. A moving target for all who play catchup, with a prodigy founder, hedge fund money as a safety net and a head start of two years.

Getting one's head around it.

But of course Sarah is right, there is a lot of confusion about what *existing* real–world problems blockchains might help with – and which not.

Complemented by the expectable ignorance about what *new* things it can be used for, which is the even more exciting part and far from fully figured out yet.

It's a bit bad even among developers, consultants and managers tasked to evaluate and chart strategy. Well, this book won't tell anyone you're reading it.

The hardest part is, to get a handle on what block-chains actually *do*. Because it's unlike what came before. One has to get used to it and learn how to reason about its application. There are a lot of bad analogies out there for what the blockchain is like; and they can be very mis-leading.

We'll be coming at it from different angles. Even a tiny bit of code.

But if you want to memorize just one thing:

> ## Blockchains are about guarantee of execution.

That is the *smarts* of smart contracts: they *will* execute.

They are not just a program waiting for someone to run it or not. They are not just legal text expressed as a program (they are almost never that currently).

And that means, blockchains are *not* just a new way of storing data. The main reason why people want to believe this, is because it keeps the hope alive that it's easy to understand.

But blockchains are *not* just Distributed Ledger Technology (DLT) as even the EU calls them officially now.

And this matters, because if you look for a good use case for blockchain tech in the *database* corner, inevitably you'll end up with an idea that instead should be solved using one of the awe-inspiring, mature, robust, scalable and fast database systems out there. And then Sarah has to find a polite way to navigate your enthusiasm.

Knock, knock ...

Take the Red Pill

Discover something world changing.

If you want to create digital cash, there's a challenge: everything that's digital can be copied, at virtually no cost. But your cash will be worthless if anybody can just multiply it.

The inventors of Bitcoin found a solution. To pre–empt copying, Bitcoin copies everything. Instead of trying to prevent multiplication, Bitcoin's makers went into the opposite extreme: everything is copied to everyone who makes part of the system. As a starting point. And that worked.

> ### Bitcoins are digital but
> ### *cannot be copied.*

This crazy approach made new things possible. Digital cash that does not need a bank is just the first of many use cases. In more general terms:

Blockchains introduce
digital scarcity.

Ethereum built on the ground that Bitcoin broke, generalizing the invention and taking it one step further:

Ethereum programs
cannot be stopped.[*]

And because these newly discovered principles work no-matter if they are legal or not, some now argue:

Blockchains are like
a *force of nature.*

You can 'ban' them but not make them go away. Law might have to adapt to a new reality.

So follow the white rabbit, ogle the red pill of truth about what will happen to commerce, banking and law in the near future. It brings about changes that are hard to find realistic.

But, who would have found a prediction of the Internet realistic?

---

[*] It's relative. With a lot of money, hardware or charisma you can.

Don't get put off by the current hard limitations of blockchains. People are very aware of them and are working on the next generation of the technology.

Blockchains will be to finance what the Internet was to music and video.

Blockchains may be the finance industry's *BitTorrent*. This is a *decentralized protocol* that is still used today to load music 'free'.

> ## You can't
> ## defeat a protocol.

A protocol is different from a program in that it just describes *how the communication should work*, which allows for different ways to implement it, e.g. using different programming languages.

Accordingly, there are many different BitTorrent clients that can all communicate with each other, because they follow the same communication protocol: BitTorrent.

Same with Ethereum. It's essentially a protocol.

The entertainment industry invested fortunes to take the BitTorrent *network* down, but for technical reasons alone, they can't. Because, as opposed to *Napster*,[3] the BitTorrent protocol is *decentralized*. Napster was centralized, its protocol involved central server hubs, through which it was taken out by legal means, fast.

---

3   Naspter was the first popular system to, well, share music.

With the BitTorrent, Bitcoin and Ethereum networks you don't have that – centralized servers – and that's no coincidence. They consist of thousands of equal nodes[4] and it does not matter if some, or even a lot, go down.

Every blockchain node is equal.

The only thing you can do to try to take over, is trying to get a majority of nodes. Or more exactly a majority of computational power.

Decentralization pre-empts outside control.

There is no hierarchy to dock into, so outside hierarchies have a harder time to assert control.

Now, Bitcoin is limited in what it can do, which is why Ethereum was invented. Because it turns out that the blockchain's real power goes beyond vanilla payments. It could do a lot of stuff free that banks earn billions for. It should even be more robust and allow for – gasp – yet more complex products.

---

4   Nodes are what the network connects. A 'node' is usually one computer, no matter the size. But more strictly, it's one instance of a client program running. This could be multiple times on one and the same computer. In which case that computer would be said to host multiple nodes. To the blockchain, only the clients matters, and not wether a client shares the hardware with another client.

This reality is dawning upon the financial sector. And all brands in banking are working now to find out what this revolution is all about. They hire smart people and throw a lot of money at 'proof of concepts'.

But ultimately, understanding the Internet better, helped a CD press company only so much in 1999. The Internet put an end to the need for a physical (entertainment–) data medium. And likewise, banking will have to change as the blockchain makes their role as *intermediaries for financial transactions* largely redundant.

For centuries, banks had succeeded in reducing the costs of transactions and earning money from this service. It was predictable since the 70's that it was going towards zero and banks accordingly tried new things. Now we're here.

A less dramatic truth is that banking is looking for serious change ever since 2008, because hundreds of thousands of bankers have been let go and someone has to do their work, while new regulations add ever more pressure to gain productivity. The sector would chase anything right now that promises a new hope. Along came blockchains.

Add to that how the North Koreans are running circles around *SWIFT*[5] and it becomes plausible that bankers are on board.[6]

---

5   The Society for Worldwide Interbank Financial Telecommunication enables international money transfers between banks. Note how this is a *communication* service.

6   The North Korea heist was not really SWIFT's fault. It's an unfair perception. You could steal blockchain money the exact same way.

But Richard Brown,[7] an ex–colleague and founder of *R3 CEV*[8] rightly asks, why *"something invented to replace an industry should become the savior of that industry?"*[9]

That's spot on, however the vision for the *distributed ledger* product *Corda*[10] that R3 proposes is merely *"a single global logical ledger [that] is authoritative for all agreements between firms."* It does not include smart contracts[11] and as they say themselves, is not a blockchain.[12]

And so in a way, R3 and the 60 big banks in their consortium seem undecided as to whether they really want to jump. Reducing honest mistakes, as a distributed ledger could, has huge benefits. But the true innovative potential is powered by real *digital assets* and smart contracts.

Blockchains bring about automated Law.

Law may get hit even harder than banking – or it may turn out to be the blockchain's paper industry! Like, the paperless office did not happen, office printers arrived in time.

The nature of making legal contracts will likely change dramatically and litigation might take a back seat to *prevention:* because a blockchain gives you the guarantee that a

---

7   Richard writes some of the best and most accessible fintech stuff about blockchains, tackling profound questions – https://gendal.me

8   R3 CEV – http://r3cev.com

9   https://gendal.me/2016/04/05/introducing-r3-corda-a-distributed-ledger-designed-for-financial-services/

10 Corda – http://r3cev.com/s/corda-introductory-whitepaper-final.pdf

11 R3 prefer Barclay's re–definition of 'smart contract' that antithetically favors legal settlement over self–execution (see pg. 154). One therefore finds claims that Corda was supporting smart contracts.

12 *"we are not building a blockchain"* – ibid.

contract will execute – including moving assets and money – exactly as cod(ifi)ed.

Two key players in the Ethereum community, *Gavin Wood* of *EthCore*[13] and *Casey Kuhlman* of *Monax*,[14] were coming from this very angle originally: how to translate law into programs.

We will need lawyers who know how to program, or programmers who know law. And we will need fewer people who think hard about written prose to find out what could be supposed it might have been meant to mean.

If I was a lawyer I'd brush up my BASIC[15] right now. That might do.[16]

Research into 'scripted law' – legal texts expressed as computer programs – is hard to find. It seems to be happening mostly on the fringes of efforts that are focussed on the automated creation of normal, human readable legal texts.[17] These initiatives are precursors of proper legal 'contracts–as–programs', laying the ground with their focus on the modularity of law. And as an organic aside, they speculate about ways to create output that is smart contract code instead of legal prose.

---

13 EthCore created an Ethereum client for IoT, see pg. 77.

14 Monax is a blockchain tool maker, see pg. 75.

15 A 60's beginner's programming language, kept alive by Microsoft.

16 In fact, a lawyer who read the draft of this book came back to me laughing as this was exactly what he had started doing.

17 James Hazard's Common Accord – http://www.commonaccord.org
Christoper Clack's Smart Contract Templates –
http://www0.cs.ucl.ac.uk/staff/C.Clack/SCT2016.pdf
Beware these are *not* smart contracts, see pg. 177.

Automated collaboration, even between machines.

Blockchain technology will allow for new things to happen in traditional commerce, the *sharing economy*[18] and the *Internet of Things* (IoT)[19]. Fringe markets, collaborative organizations, self-driving cars, will all benefit. As will every domain where progress can happen by sharing and trading in a more reliable way.

> ## Blockchains enable machines to do business directly with other machines.

Without a proxy that checks on them or signs things off. Because it allows for *negotiations and binding agreements between parties that do not know each other.* And who accordingly, also don't know if they can trust each other.

This is the dawn of machine–to–machine commerce (M2M) and new markets in a plethora of niches where the overhead of doing business was just not worth it in the past.

In the domain of governance, blockchains should allow to 'scale trust:' we should see *reputation systems* emerge that allow for communities to grow beyond the level where natural trust between individuals works as the foundation of interaction.

---

18   A philosophy and business model based on people renting out to each other what they don't currently use. Usually supported by web sites and apps – see e.g. http://ouishare.net

19   Home devices like fridges, scales, thermostats with Internet access and/or communicating directly amongst each other; but also industrial machinery like jet engines phoning health metrics home 24/7.

The overhead that is eliminated would usually not be on the happy path, but in dealing with the question of what should happen when something goes wrong, or someone turns out to cheat – or just resorts to self-serving subjectivity.

Or if you know your counter-party just has no conscience at all, cannot be punished and knows it – because it's a machine.

> **Blockchains prevent things from going wrong *in the first place*.**

To a shocking degree, they can make sure everyone plays by the rules, as agreed upon when entering the deal.

And that can change a lot.

We are early.

Why should Visa be worried about a technology that can't do a hundredths of the throughput they need.

And understandably, Uber can't be bothered to look deeper after seeing blockchains don't even scale, at this point, to what they need *now*.

Bankers have done their homework, understand the limitations and have decided to give blockchains a timeframe of two to three years to mature.

Some are announcing ground breaking initiatives, some say that if the stuff really turns out that great, they'll be perfectly happy to splash a billion on the winning contender then.

For programmers it's about artificial 'life'.

That code on the blockchain is *guaranteed* to execute independent of its creator and deployer makes it different. This aspect is easy to overlook and is honey to developers.

People sometimes criticize the bigotry of the world-saving talk that can be observed in the space. The counter-weight to that is unabashed greed and currency speculation obviously. You have both types in the community and Ethereum is lucky to have a better balance than Bitcoin. But it seems to be easy to miss that a number of people at the very core are in it for the love of the tech.

Take the fascination of code, per se. There is thrill for us in a green-on-black terminal screen, seeing a program build or execute, logs rattling by. We love thinking up stuff, finding a formula and coding it so it runs with predictable as well as surprising results, taking over chores or allowing for something new.

It doesn't have to be AI but it always feels a bit like it. And we are talking about 'normal' programs here.

> ### With blockchains, programs take on a life of their own.

The fascination of bringing something to life is why viruses had their allure, agents that replicate, travel and, in our minds, explore, autonomously. Blockchains take that one huge step further. Code that not only can take on the unknown – but code that will execute for sure, on thousands of computers at the same time, de facto detached from any one physical representation, being everywhere and no-where 'living' in cyberspace.

Code not dependent on the lucky circumstance that people fire it up because they find it useful. It's the difference between Tron[20] and Crom, once you get it – pure adrenalin. Code that cannot be stopped, by design.

Well, yes, like *SkyNet*.[21] Or *The DAO*.[22]

Of course we will be able to dream up new things with this. The only sad thing about Ethereum being that it has no *Forth*[23]-like language like Bitcoin.

This fascination will drive adoption among devs. Programmers want to work with this, they are learning it in their free time. This is an important parameter.

---

20 A daring 80's movie inspired by Pong. You thought a Transformers movie was a crazy idea. If you know it, watch it again. It's bolder than you remember.

21 The main AI enemy in the Terminator movie series.

22 See pg. 286

23 Forth is an awesome 70's programming language where everything is piled up onto one stack and written backwards.

Hello, World!

To make a point, here is a very small Ethereum program written in *Solidity*, the language of choice that smart contracts are written in:

```solidity
contract Hello {
  event Log(bytes32 msg);
  function Hello() {
    Log("Hello, World!");
  }
}
```

This is a minimal Ethereum *contract*. Obviously this contract has nothing to do with law, it's simply a script.[24]

If you deploy this script to the Ethereum network, it will log "Hello, World!" to the global Ethereum *receipts* log and that's it. It won't ever do anything after that, but the log it creates is somewhat special.

---

24 Scripts are short programs. While big programs can have millions of lines and are often *compiled* to machine language before being executed, scripts usually have from one to a few thousand lines and are often written in languages that are *interpreted* one word after the other while being executed. Scripts can be very low level, dealing with files, or very high level and expressing business logic.

This script is not really a *smart contract*, but in Ethereum we call all scripts *contracts*. And while more complex scripts can in fact bind parties into self-enforcing agreements, this script does not affect anyone else.

The special thing about its output is that it's indisputable that it happened. You get a log, confirmed to have been seen by currently 7,500 computers out there that run Ethereum clients. And they confirm that you expressed "Hello, World!" at a given time. In fact, many of them are getting paid, in a way, for collectively giving you this attestation.

Printing "Hello, World!" to the screen is a trope in CS, basically every computer language book starts out with this.

But our Hello! Is different: it's *really* going out to the *world!* It doesn't go to your screen but instead executes on thousands of computers all over the globe.

> ## Writes to a blockchain are global and permanent.

Plus, its output *and* the program itself cannot be altered after the fact – they are '*immutable*' – and permanently stored in the blockchain, with a timestamp. To get the program to run, you also have to sign it first. The same as with any data and parameters you send to the blockchain.

Taken together –

- ♦ immutability,
- ♦ permanence,
- ♦ timestamp,
- ♦ signature and
- ♦ global availability

have the effect that:

Data and programs on the blockchain are auditable.

Something written to the blockchain really has every feature an auditor wants, or a judge for that matter.

In the near future, regulators and judges will pick up on that. The *Silkroad*[25] verdict was actually a milestone on the way there, because digital signatures were accepted as proof during the trial. And the European Union[26] is researching if the burden of regulatory compliance can be reduced for financial institutions by accepting blockchain values as trust-worthy without additional trail of proofs.

This example *is* on the database side, where people are excited about the *auditability* of a blockchain. And because

---

25 Ross Ulbricht was sent to prison for life without parole based on the evidence of digital signatures. He was busted for running an anonymous marketplace, Silkroad, where people could pay each other in Bitcoin and that was used for dealing drugs.

26 The Directorate-General of the European Commission for Financial Stability, Financial Services and Capital Markets Union (FISMA).

of the permanence and immutability – the perception that today's blockchains never drop anything ever written to them – they are also called *ledgers*.

People love that term because it's a centuries old banking term that gives a cozy feeling and implies it's all really nothing new. But this is just the start, it's *not* all.

I am with *Vitalik Buterin*[27] here, the inventor of Ethereum, who finds that *"it's a ledger"*–thinking highly limiting. And it's no secret that there are marketing reasons in play at this point why some people think it's beneficial to reduce blockchains to a ledger.

Rethinking Security.

That we can write a script and have it run on thousands of computers of people who don't know us poses a lot of hard security questions.

Could we spam all these friendly nodes? Crash the entire network with a buggy script? And in fact:

> Public blockchains introduce
> *a new type of security.*

The basic premise is that all nodes control each other all the time and they can do that because they know exactly what every other node *should* hold as truth at any given time. If all nodes agree, this is called *consensus*.

---

27 Vitalik also writes great stuff, very clear thoughts in very clear language, e.g. at https://blog.ethereum.org/author/vitalik-buterin/ Not all of it technical and usually highly relevant to the field. He made his name as writer of Bitcoin Magazine as a teen and it shows.

> ## Who doesn't agree – is simply kicked off the network.

That everyone can agree on the input is because all input is digitally signed.

But there is more to it, both Bitcoin and Ethereum introduce *economic incentives* to secure their networks.

If you are interested in details about the Hello, World! source code check out the appendix, pg. 323.

Hello, 5th Dimension!

Your bitcoins are worth something not only because no one in the past could just copy and duplicate them, and you can't duplicate them now. But because the rules of the Bitcoin network guarantee that also *in the future* they cannot be copied.

This reach into the fourth dimension, time, is of the essence, characterizing a blockchain.

Ethereum goes a step further and allows you to *program* the future, to implement rules governing the array of possibilities that fan out from the present.

Programs always kind-of do that but usually they are stoppable and rarely do they move money in non-revocable ways. Ethereum smart contracts are all about that. And in fact they should not be used for anything less, because of Ethereum's hard capacity and performance limitations.

To rephrase that most important thing to understand:

Smart contracts
will execute. *

It's about being able to program what should happen, in a way that can't be changed nor stopped. Except – and that's the asterisk – if everyone who runs a node agrees to stop the chain. Thousands of people in the case of Ethereum or Bitcoin.

And that's the differentiating part, not the ledger thing. Ethereum is a really awful database, there are ledgers that are literally a million times faster. It's not distributed, it's decentralized.

But this *guarantee of execution* is new.

Say you wanted to take out a life insurance on your favorite online game character.

Let's imagine the game provider has a web site ranking all avatars in the game. And let's say one can be sure that if one checks a certain web page and the character's account number is not displayed anymore, that means the character is 'dead.'

Ignoring the blockchain for a moment, you could make a contract with anybody that would offer to guarantee you a payment of, say $1,000 in case that happens: your character has died, proven by his name disappearing from that page.

You pay a small fee, maybe $10. When your character dies, say within a year, that person is to pay you $1,000.

Now, if they don't cough up their payout, you could go to court, right. The judge would check a piece of paper where you spelled out the contract, signed by both of you. Then she would go to the web site or ask for other proof that your avatar died. Ideally the contract would have been notarized. So the judge can trust that you show her the correct contract, as it was, when it was signed and doesn't have to trust you.

But the contract may still turn out to mean different things to different people. So therefore, now you try to persuade the judge of your view.

Except of course all this wouldn't happen because $1,000 is not worth the legal cost and hassle.

And that's a sufficient reason for such an insurance market not to exist.

The difference that a blockchain can make, is that it can *guarantee that the payment will happen*, with absolute certainty.

How that should work?

Basically by making sure that

1. *every transaction going into the system is signed and*
2. *everyone in the network executes it to completion.*

That is the basic principle that ties contracts and payments together in a new and emergent way.

It is the very basis underlying Ethereum.

ETHEREUM

"A universal platform with internal programming language, so that everyone could write any app."

Vitalik Buterin

What is Ethereum?

Ethereum is the world computer.

Ethereum is the promise of interactivity between millions of smart contracts, working together in unpredictable ways to exchange information, create marketplaces and extend new types of services.

It is accessible by anyone. Anyone can upload programs and data and execute any program deployed to it by anybody.

And, on a side note, 'world computer' is an oddly centralized perspective. The one computer for the entire globe. The centralized result of complete decentralization. Keep an eye on this ambiguity.

Ethereum is a blockchain.

There are as many definitions for what a blockchain is as there are blockchain experts, minus one (I witnessed two agreeing once). We'll get into that in a Berlin minute.

Bitcoin was the first blockchain, now there are roughly a thousand projects trying to improve on it. While Bitcoin is focussed on payments, Ethereum is a programmable, *general purpose* blockchain and by far the most powerful out there that can be used today. Almost every team on blockchain hackathons these days uses Ethereum.

Ethereum is general-purpose.

Where Bitcoin is *intentionally* dumbed down in its capabilities, the scripts run by Ethereum are *stateful*[28] and *Turing-complete.*[29]

This simply means that Ethereum 'contracts' have memory that they will remember the next time they are called and that they can have loops. They look and work a lot like *objects* in object oriented programming.

> ## Ethereum smart contracts have code and memory.

Bitcoin transactions execute only once, so have no need for this type of memory, and they can't have loops.

Plus, Ethereum comes with a comfortable programming language, called *Solidity*, that the contracts are written in.

---

28 'State' in CS means any datapoint or any amount of data. 'Stateful' means that data is remembered by something for some time.

29 All modern programming languages are Turing-complete, from which follows that what can be programmed in one language can be programmed in any other. It just looks and performs differently. The Bitcoin blockchain as a whole is Turing-complete, too, but its individual scripts that drive its transactions, are not, as they do not allow for loops.

Bitcoin has this awesome Forth-like language called *Script*. But it is used in a very special, limiting way and just no match to a complete language.

With Bitcoin, what one can program is a multi-signature transaction that only executes when two people give their consent to it. You can make it two out of two, or two out of three, or two or two others out of four. But that's really it. Any logic beyond that has to be programmed *off-chain* and has to be tied into these primitives. Which kind of works.

But with Ethereum you are free to really program, anything, and your scripts running on the blockchains can be applications that own money and never stop. It's purpose is to be able to do everything any other blockchain can, and then some.

Ethereum is the blockchain of blockchains.

And it does deliver now and likely will get even better – much more versatile, scalable and faster – in the future.

You can program prediction markets,[30] reputations systems,[31] new digital currencies[32] or a land title registry[33] all directly on the blockchain. And all that is being done.

Ethereum's inventor, Vitalik Buterin, likes to stress that Ethereum's *stateful scripts* are the more powerful difference

30 Augur – https://www.augur.net, Gnosis – https://www.gnosis.pm
31 Backfeed – http://backfeed.cc
32 Digital Currencies – see pg. 70
33 ChromaWay – http://chromaway.com

and that the talk about the Turing-completeness is over-blown.[34]

But as with all general-purpose solutions, there is a price.

And for Ethereum this is speed and capacity. Even though it is much faster than Bitcoin, it is still way too slow to program an entire system on top of it. Especially calculation intensive stuff is much too expensive to be run on the Ethereum *mainnet*. The mainnet being the one network where the 'real' cryptocurrencies reside, as opposed to the *testnets* or any of the private blockchain networks that work identically but by definition do not carry any 'real' value.

To build a useful application, much logic will be executed *off-chain* at this point. And as has often been the case with IT, future, faster hardware may solve a sizable part of this problem.

Ethereum is a platform for decentralized applications, smart contracts and decentralized, autonomous organizations.

That's a mouthful – basically it is about programs being unstoppable, incorruptible and able to make irreversible payments, which can be used to craft business agreements, a.k.a. contracts, that can be said to *execute themselves*. Without needing banks, notaries or lawyers, even in cases where things turn out very different from what was expected.

---

34 There is an argument to be made that Turing-completeness might not be necessary for blockchain programs at this point. See pg. 209.

Eventually it's about the new opportunity to build self-sustaining, economic entities that 'live' on the chain and offer real–world services: the *DAOs*.

The contract is the money.

Or, the contract itself holds the money. It's hard to grok in the beginning, and extremely powerful.

A contract on the blockchain is akin to writing a contract on a $100 note and ripping it apart, so that only when both parties come together again can the money be pieced together and spent.

In yet other words, the *contract* and the *escrow account* of a transaction are literally one and the same.

There is a clear hierarchy involved: first you need a platform – e.g. Ethereum – to execute *decentralized code* on. Which can be called a *smart contract* if it is used to express an agreement and transfers value. And an elaborate form of a *smart contract* is the *decentralized, autonomous organization* (DAO), which is programmed to perpetuate its existence, accordingly consists of smart contracts that are designed to never stop and that has its own funds that it manages according to only the rules programmed into it.

Ethereum is a global, public, somewhat anonymous network of computers that anyone can join.

The network is literally decentralized, in the sense that no one can dictate their decisions to its community.

> ## Ethereum is free.
> ## No one owns it.

The software is free as well. You can start taking part in it right away.

See the appendix, pg. 331ff. on how to install a client.

Ethereum is a massively many-times mirrored, global computer.

Aeron Buchanan, one of the unsung heroes of Ethereum, likes to call it *"the least efficient, yet most open and reliable way to compute."*

Usually, for anything else but blockchains, a network is put to good use by distributing *disparate* chunks of the workload between nodes, to get the work done faster. Not so with blockchains.

Blockchains do *symmetric* computation.

Every node in a blockchain stores and computes the *same* data.

The nodes even execute the exact same calculations at roughly the exact same moment in time. Give or take some seconds.

That's the main trick.

And this is what 'synchronizing' means: your client downloads all the blocks and ancillary data from other clients in the network and calculates through *everything* that has ever been posted to (and accepted into) the Ethereum network. From the very first block.

That's right: every transaction that was ever made, every contract that was ever invoked, is re-lived by your client. By this, it makes sure that the data it is receiving is consistent *and* double checks the global *state* of the Ethereum network. It has to trust its sources for *some* things, but relatively little. And because it's only few things it has to believe, it can crosscheck with a lot of peers on whether they agree.

Programmers call all or part of the data that a program deals with 'state', e.g. the contents of a variable, or an entire database. It usually changes over time. But if an algorithm runs multiple times with the exact same input, it should end up with the same state as result every time. This is called *determinism* and is mostly also true for programs.

And not only should there be agreement at the end, but really in every single computational step. So if multiple identical computers start the same program with the same input, they should likewise all end up with the same state as result. Which is the fundamental premise that blockchains are built upon.

And so, if everything goes right, your client will arrive after synching at the exact same *world state* as every other Ethereum node, calculated everything anyone ever did on the chain from the starting point, called the *genesis block*.

The world state being the totality of all bits of data in the system. *But:*

> Everyone calculating everything does not scale. *Not at all.*

Meaning, the data on that network cannot become arbitrarily big. At some not too far away point in history, the tail of blocks will get a bit long. So the more nodes make good use of Ethereum, the longer will every new node have to work to get in. Ethereum will have to change, and that was clear from the very beginning.

But as it is, the fact that every Ethereum client does that, re-calculating everything, is what makes Ethereum secure.

And again, the outcome of the world state is indisputable and trustworthy because *every transaction that comes in and triggers a change to the world state is cryptographically signed by the account owner that the transaction originates from.*

In other words, from the dawn of time, every single change to the global world state of the Ethereum network has been signed off by the person owning the sender account of the transaction effecting the change. In effect:

> ## Because everything is signed, there is no need to trust.

Importantly, every computation executed on the block-chain is by a *signed program*, too, as all code on the blockchain – i.e. the transaction scripts *themselves* – are deployed to the blockchain as signed input parameters to a transaction.

And as a result, the chain of all these transactions leads to a current global state that all Ethereum clients agree upon to be The Truth™ because they all saw the signatures of every single element involved.

As for the scaling, well, lots of smart guys are breaking their heads about it. Should be there, soon. Lot's of tricks to pull before we run out. Everyone has a rough idea of how *sharding*[35] is going to work. Vitalik Buterin, *Vlad Zamfir*, Gavin Wood and *Dominic Williams* pursue their competing approaches in different business set ups. But no-one *knows*. Shocking enough.

---

35 Sharding means splitting world state up into multiple chunks, usually one chunk – 'shard' – per machine in a computer cluster. With Ethereum it will mean splitting the world state up into multiple sub chains, each running on many nodes.

Ethereum is the most performant and productive blockchain.

Ethereum is the fastest platform for decentralized applications.

Simply because there is no faster one that can do real decentralized applications. And the speed with which deals can be finalized on Ethereum is what may revolutionize trading.

Blockchains that claim to be faster usually simply have no (on–chain) smart contracts at all.

But most of all:

It's *fast to write* decentralized applications for Ethereum.

Which is often a more crucial metric than how fast a system executes. Time to market, programmer hours billed – those things can make or break a project. And therefore, many languages and development environments trade speed of execution in for speed of development. *Java*[36] is a prime example. It took a decade to approach the execution speed of *C++*[37] but it was worth it.

---

36 Java – one of the most popular, general–purpose program languages in commercial IT, created to be robust and useful across many different platforms.

Looking at some simple Ethereum code examples, you realize how incredibly much you get for free and how powerful some tiny scripts can be when running on Ethereum.

But we will look at the hefty downsides.

Ethereum has on-chain smart contracts.

It's worth noting that a defining feature of Ethereum is to have the code *on-chain*. This means that programs are really stored in the blocks and not just something pointing to them with the actual code sitting somewhere else.

There are different ways to link code to a blockchain, just like any data can be *linked* into the chain without actually becoming part of it.

E.g. one can take contract programming off-chain entirely and store but *hashes*[38] of the code into the blockchain. The smart contracts then become invisible for the blockchain itself. But one can program special clients that know how to find the actual code and are programmed to execute it after making sure it matches the hash in the chain.

Many blockchain projects propose this because it allows one to skip a lot of work, promise nice performance metrics and have an easier time to design a scaling blockchain.

However, Joe Latone, the blockchain pioneer at IBM agrees that:

---

37 C++ – the dominant general–purpose programming language before Java arrived, geared towards a slightly deeper level of system programming.

38 Hashes are used as a form of ids or pointers in this case, see pg. 118.

> ## Having the contracts *on-chain* might be the killer difference.

Similar to serving a web page via *FTP*[39] or *HTTP*:[40] You can program a web server using FTP. It was around long before HTTP and nobody did that. IBM even made an experiment back then to test that out. It might have worked but was just not productive. That's when IBM decided to use HTTP.

Ethereum can be called Bitcoin 2.0.

Bitcoin maximalists don't like that. Vitalik does not agree either, he feels this was like *"calling a smart phone a pocket calculator 2.0."*

One could even argue that it's as wrong as calling a *calculator factory* a calculator 2.0, because one can program something like Bitcoin on top of Ethereum. It happens all the time now with people issuing new *tokens* that have some special-purpose, programmed and living on the Ethereum mainnet. Those tokens are in effect new cryptocurrencies, every single one of them.

---

39 File Transfer Protocol of the Internet, the default for transferring files, dating from 1971, 20 years before the the World Wide Web was implemented.

40 The Internet protocol for web pages. The world wide web is a vision from the 1930's, implemented in the 1990's introducing both a new language, HTML, and a new protocol HTTP. From the start, older formats and protocols where supported by browsers, too, namely FTP, NNTP, and local files. But web sites took off thanks to HTTP and the HTML it transports.

But on the other hand, technically and as a matter of complexity, Ethereum is quite similar to Bitcoin.

It's not like a calculator vs. its factory, not even as far apart as a calculator and a smart phone.

Ethereum has its focus on smart contracts instead of being exclusively a digital currency. And as part of that, Ethereum transactions can be way more sophisticated than Bitcoin's: full fledged, high language programs, some many thousand lines long, which can call each other, almost ad infinitum. Bitcoin only allows for a very small number of cryptic bytes per transaction.

And with Ethereum, a good deal of work went into making sure everything also stops at some point, addressing the *Halting Problem* (pg. 206).

Ethereum is SkyNet.

We have this running gag that Ethereum is SkyNet. Because Bitcoin had been said to be intentionally not offering Turing completeness, lest it could become SkyNet. Along comes Vitalik and proposes just that, let's have a Turing-complete blockchain!

However, the way that the Ethereum network of synchronized nodes works together – to create trust, or rather, to substitute for the lack of it, for a vast array of business cases – has effects so emergent, it's reminiscent of AI.

Already there are passionate debates flaring up of how to best rein in the coming emergence. The unintended consequences people anticipate will look somewhat like the 2010 Flash Crash[41] – just in more tangible domains.

---

41 A trillion-dollar stock market crash, which lasted for approximately 36 minutes, allegedly caused by a single spoofing day trader's bots.

Blockchains will be a great way for drones to navigate right–of–way, implement irrigation strategies – or to do other things in concert, with sadder payloads.

The material change to the network that was proposed to revert The DAO heist (see pg. 286) showed how not even the core developer community was able to shut parts of the network down. Instead, *Ethereum Classic* emerged as unintended consequence (pg. 293). They tried. But they could not kill their own beast.

So if one day it's about averting the self-destruction of our planet, maybe we can all agree and switch off the *miners* (pg. 157). But anything less, there's probably going to be some disgruntled maximalist who will keep one node running.

And in fact, the resilience of a blockchain network *is* fascinating.

> ## A Blockchain survives
> ## as long as one node stays up.

When developing, it's quite amazing what can be observed when running a testnet into the ground: even after catastrophic failure of almost all nodes, if only one survives, it will keep the network state and over time re-supply all crashed nodes when they come back up, so the network on the whole will continue without loss of data.

No outside recovery action is necessary to facilitate this. This doggedness is a direct result from the basic functions of the blockchain protocol.

So, if you try to take out a blockchain you have to be sure you take out every and all nodes. Or it will re-emerge like Perseus' Hydra. Adds a pest-like quality to the SkyNet meme.

Ethereum is an altcoin.

Meaning, it's another me-too improving on Bitcoin. The difference is, it really does improve. And it really succeeded like no other.

As with all the other altcoins, hard core Bitcoin guys loathed and dissed Ethereum. Even one Bitcoin fan working for Ethereum's security did.

But Ethereum really is an altcoin in how it attracts people who want to get rich quick and in how greed is accepted as honorable motivation, which can get in the way of community building and research some times.

It had originally been discussed to not built a native cryptocurrency into Ethereum. In which case Ethereum itself would not strictly have been an altcoin.

But there should be some form of digital currency available for smart contracts. And without the Ether presale, how should the crowdfunding have worked out.

Still, it's the implementation of a fungible digital currency that poses the gravest challenges for scalability.

Ethereum is a community.

Vitalik has embraced Open Source spirit and inclusiveness from day one.

The Ethereum Foundation got it right how they focus on developers throughout and the great vibes at the developer conference in September 2016 in Shanghai, *Devcon 2*, was testament to that.

Where Bitcoin events attracted money types and VCs too early, the Devcons manage to remain developer–centric and a hub for deep technical discussions. Most of all though they keep bringing people together who are really into the tech, and just enjoy to meet and work with each other.

It's not like there aren't strong egos and stupid decisions in the mix. But enough folks are in it neither trying to save the world nor make the quick buck but for the love of thinking and coding. Boldly going – now and then – where no one went before. Sometimes deciding for what's fun rather than what's needed. Reinventing a wheel that already existed. Call it research.

But in terms of sheer blockchain know–how it's pretty strong.

What is Ether?

Ether is the *native token* of Ethereum, its 'bitcoins'.

Ether is to Ethereum, what bitcoins are to, well, Bitcoin.

'Ethereum' is the name for the *technology*, the *client software* and the *mainnet*. 'Ether' is the *digital currency* that is hard-coded into that system.

The term 'Ethereum' remains sufficiently overloaded. Not naming Ether 'Ethereum,' is laudable progress I guess.

Ether is what you pay with for using Ethereum.

This is the official definition of Ether: it's the currency in which to pay the fee to be allowed to run your calculations, make your transactions and store your data on the blockchain that is the Ethereum mainnet. That's no theory, it's really how it works, the details are surprisingly complex (pg. 206) with ultra-nano payment for that built into the deepest level of the system.

Whenever you make a transaction – i.e. move Ether, or execute a smart contract – you as *the caller* of it have to pay the network at large for its execution. In a fascinating way this should back the price of Ether in a similar fashion to how normal money (fiat' as blockchain people like to call it) is backed nowadays by the promise that the government will accept it to pay your taxes in.

The amounts to be payed are small but might in the future rise as there is a market system built into the transaction handling of Ethereum: when calculation power gets scarce – which is not the case at all right now – prices per transactions will rise and miners can freely decide to pick those transactions that come with the offer of the highest price for their execution. This *fee market* creates a demand for Ether. Makes a lot of sense.

Ether was sold to crowd-fund Ethereum.

Now, Ether were also used to crowd-fund Ethereum, and is used to reward miners, the people who actually run the computers of the network, much like it works in Bitcoin.

A lot of people bought Ether for $0.30 in hopes that it will appreciate, and some sold it at $20. That made a lot of sense, too.

When you busy some of your computers as *miners* (pg. 157), that gives you a chance to earn some Ether as reward now and then. This reward exists because without miners, there would be no Ethereum mainnet. Nobody could make any new transactions. With too few miners, it would be really easy to take it over.

Current development of Ethereum is largely funded by the Ethereum Foundation's Ether that was pre-mined, i.e. simply created out of thin air and hard-coded into the Ethereum network when it was started. From the get go with funding of development in mind.

Only the mainnet has the real Ether.

Both the Ethereum and the Bitcoin *software* are used to run *one public network* each, called the mainnet. Only the Ethereum mainnet has the real Ether. Just as only the Bitcoin mainnet has the real bitcoins.

There are *testnets* for both Bitcoin and Ethereum, which are technically identical to the respective mainnets almost to the last byte. The relevant difference is that by public consensus, the testnet 'Ethers' and 'bitcoins' are not 'real' and not worth anything.

Users are asked to not sell them or speculate in them and they can be obtained for free[42] – for testing.

It's a hilarious reminder of how the value of anything, even and especially cryptocurrencies like Bitcoin and Ethereum, is completely dependent on what people decide to assume.

Crypto is fiat.

Oh, did I write that. Oh no, and now I can't delete it, cr*p, because the book is on blockchain!

Ether might not become a widely used digital currency.

Ether will lose its special implementation in Ethereum in the future, if not its special status. From Ethereum 2.0, Ether will on the technical level be (re-)implemented to

---

42 Ether Camp testnet faucet – https://morden.ether.camp

then work as any other custom currency on top of Ethereum works. Like our *HelloCoin* above. Maybe a little more robustly.

Bitcoin still enjoys a visible lead as cryptocurrency of choice, even though Ether has caught up admirably.

Still, if the Bitcoin and Ethereum camps would have to agree on something, it would be Bitcoin.

The reason is ignorance on the side of the Bitcoin community, which for a long while predicted Ethereum could not work in the first place and now often still sees it as unworthy upstart. The core Ethereum people on the other hand, almost universally came from Bitcoin and continue to appreciate Bitcoin for the reasons they got into it in the first place.

No matter how wrong the Bitcoin hardcore may be, and how irrational, the state of affairs today is that Bitcoin is the king of the cryptocurrency space. And it's a network-effect market. Bitcoin is becoming somewhat mainstream, Ether is not known outside the bubble.

And now there is Zcash which has attributes that neither Bitcoin nor Ethereum can match. The market might settle for either of them as 'the' cryptocurrency.

On the other hand, Ethereum allows anyone to implement indefinitely many cryptocurrencies. This will strengthen Ether into which those new currencies will be convertible by default.

Which is a different network effect that Bitcoin and Zcash don't enjoy.

Ethereum smart contracts might be using Bitcoin. Or Zcash.

Right now it doesn't look like it, but there already exists a Bitcoin client, programmed in Ethereum, *BTC Relay*,[43] that allows for the verification of Bitcoin transactions from Ethereum. It's at this point forbiddingly expensive only because it is lacking the critical mass of users to cover its fix run time cost. So as it stands, it is only interesting for super high value transactions. But this can change at any moment, as soon as a business comes along that finds the cost proposition of BTC Relay attractive as is and breaks down the current price barrier for everyone else by just using it.

Down the road, for Ethereum smart contracts to deal in bitcoins, or Zcash, might become as common as paying in Ether.

There are good reasons for wanting to have more than one blockchain going forward. It will be healthier for the entire field. If one chain runs into a serious problem, it won't bring down the entire domain. Bitcoin will be safer than Ethereum for a while, because it will change much less, and has had much more time to mature, with all the good and bad that goes with that.

Finally, the Ether exchange price might go through a phase of volatility for a while, following similar patterns as Bitcoin did, before stabilizing – if ever. It certainly has crazier headlines right now, as a consequence of the more interesting things one can do with it. The currency with less volatility is better suited as means of payment.

So it *could* turn out that Bitcoin will remain the crypto-currency of choice. It has the singular focus on it, is robust

---

43 Joseph Chow's BTC Relay – http://btcrelay.org

and has the name recognition. Or Zcash might take the crown, likewise for its singular focus, being firmly based on Bitcoin's battle tested basis and offering true privacy.

What is Ethereum Not?

Ethereum is not a better solution to every database problem. Not at all.

Ethereum is many *magnitudes* slower than today's databases.

For almost all use cases (pg. 224). It has a hugely – but really massively – lower capacity than databases. And the mainnet, by design, is infinitely less confidential.

That it *can* be *much faster* than today's systems is true exclusively in a holistic view, when its capability to *finalize and settle deals* is pulled into the equation.

Many 'blockchain' ideas should use a database or cloud service instead.

It's refreshing to see the creativity in many proposals what the blockchain could help with. Often times, those are actually applications for plain *cryptography*,[44] which is great, too, that people develop visions involving that now. No kidding. But –

If it doesn't need guaranteed execution, it's not a blockchain use case.

If it only uses smart contracts like database triggers, it's unlikely to justify the inconveniences of a full blockchain.

If it just uses the blockchain as a *distributed ledger*, the cost and overhead will likely not be justified. People try this currently but they often haven't calculated costs through.

If an idea can make real good use of *timestamped hashes* (pg. 191), or *identity*, *authentication* or *cryptocurrency* – it still isn't automatically a candidate for using a blockchain.

Take it from Pindar Wong, who quips the gray boxes in this chapter are worth "multi million dollars in saved grief."

Other techniques may simply be way more efficient.

Ethereum is not just a digital currency.

Ether, is an important cryptocurrency at this point, but Ethereum is much more than that.

---

44 Anything that has to do with encryption, digital signatures, hashes (pg. 118), timestamps (pg. 191).

Ethereum really is a world computer, a new breed of business logic platform. Ether is a part of that just as the ledger functionality is.

It's disruptive powers don't come from how it is such a crypto currency. It's about how it can create trust and allow for global interaction based on it.

It's full potential is not realized yet, simply because there is not much interaction at this point in time between contracts on the mainnet.

Ethereum is not fast compared to other execution environments.

Trading execution speed in for coder productivity is a common trade–off, also proposed by, say, *Python*[45] or Java.

And it is true that Ethereum is the fastest real block-chain. But ...

Ethereum can be up to 10 magnitudes slower than other platforms.

Like, 10 *billion* times slower than Java. Specifically when writing a value that you need to be sure won't get lost. Which you don't usually have to worry about when, e.g. writing a Java program.

---

45 Python – a clean looking, simple, imperative programming language that is often used to prototype ideas, or write tests for systems writ-ten in other languages. Vitalik's language of choice.

The comparison isn't fair, because the write has way more powerful attributes in Ethereum. But also weaker ones. It's just different.

However, 10 billion X is an apt predictor of the degree of disappointment you are up for, if you think you can just program a complete backend in Solidity.

The performance is like a throwback to the speed of mechanical computers. Those cog boxes made perfect sense, so does Ethereum. Things got faster, so will block-chains.

Today, smart contracts can't be crafted unthinkingly, or they get too slow and too expensive to execute. Still, a system of smart contracts can have tens of thousands of lines of codes, of which not all will be executed every time one method of it is called. That's normal for any program. In other words, a smart contracts can both be huge and still perform and be economic.

Still, the execution time now is *so* slow, it has nothing to do with what you are used to from normal scripts. The looks of Solidity are severely deceiving.

The trade-off for the productivity is so steep that it is forbidding for many – not all – projects as it is now. And because of this:

> Real products will usually mix on- and off-chain code.

Major parts of their application will be written in another language and executed not in Ethereum.

This goes without saying for the front end stuff but the issue here is the backend. Those parts will interact with Ethereum and only the code that is absolutely needed to be executed on the blockchain will be written in Solidity.

Ethereum is not anonymous nor strongly privacy-protecting.

If used right, it can yield a good degree of privacy protection. But out of the box, all transaction data, including sender account number, receiver account number and amounts transferred, are completely open and copied to every node on the network. Everyone on the planet can inspect them using one of the free, online explorers, e.g. *Ethercamp*.[46]

It's not like your name and street address is stored on the blockchain from using it. But the patterns that can arise from using Ethereum accounts can give away so much *meta information* that the owner could be identified from it.

Modern wallets offer some protection but you don't get it from Ethereum by default.

Ethereum is not as safe as Bitcoin.

As The DAO attack (pg. 286) showed, it's not even about Ethereum itself failing, it's about what you can do with it, which is a whole dimension more than with Bitcoin: people shooting their own foot with smart contract bugs, tripping up over the complexities of a new type of programming environment.

---

46 https://live.ether.camp/

Christoph Jentzsch, who programmed The DAO – which was subsequently hacked and lost $50,000,000 – is an Ethereum veteran with a university degree in theoretical and mathematical physics. He is not a seasoned coder or software system architect. But he is a smart guy who understands Ethereum. He even had professional experience as a software tester. But decentralized code can be exceedingly hard to test.

That even he can trip up, predicts that a lot of people trying their hands at smart contracts will. And it took a while, and a valuable enough target, for this particular vulnerability to be exploited. It was always there, it's impossible to know what other exploits are there.

Time will tell. And Ethereum will become safer.

Ethereum is not as ossified as Bitcoin.

The Bitcoin community is struggling to find the way forward, which is understandable because many don't want to touch a running system, which could endanger the achieved robustness.

Ethereum is creative chaos for some time to come. Good chaos. Also bad chaos but mostly good. And progressing.

Vitalik's posts[47] about Ethereum 2.0 prove that the core guys are not wed to any particular implementation but the vision. That matters because Ethereum as it turned out so far is far from perfect and new ideas keep coming up that find their way into the discussions of the developers.

---

47   https://blog.ethereum.org/2015/12/24/understanding-serenity-part-i-abstraction/ and /2015/12/28/understanding-serenity-part-2-casper/

It's not trivial to program complex systems in Ethereum.

The fact is that Ethereum has been used, almost from the start, for more complex things than it was originally designed for. This should change with Ethereum 2.0. But that is still on the drawing board.

The initial idea for Ethereum was Vitalik thinking that there should be a general purpose blockchain, *for fintech.*[48]

He had observed that all the new blockchains cropping up in 2013 were specialized to perform a number of things really well but needed to be updated, on the whole, for every *new type of transaction,* whenever a new idea or necessity came up.

Which for a blockchain means, that all node owners need to manually update. The whole network needs to be stopped and restarted.

Ethereum at its heart was the idea to make those system upgrades unnecessary.

Ethereum was made to exchange the gearbox in-flight.

But the notion of a transaction was still, basically, to transfer units of something from one account to the other.

Therefore, at the deepest level of the Ethereum *virtual machine*[49], Ethereum suffers from restrictions that looked

---

48 Financial technology, IT for banks etc.
49 A virtual machine is what actually executes a program, see pg. 199.

perfectly acceptable for fintech transactions, but hurt now that the scope has crept beyond fintech.

And for exchanging things on the fly, well you can guess that there is a price to pay and it's mostly performance. Though this will change.

Ethereum is not polished yet.

There were a lot of attacks recently on Ethereum, mostly directed on *geth*, the client implemented in *Go*.[50] The attacks exploit code and procedures in the client that were not 100% thought through. Some were embarrassing but with a system as complex as Ethereum it's bound to happen.

With every attack the clients become more robust while the vulnerabilities are fixed one by one. The *Parity* client proved to be more robust and there are 5 other alternatives to choose from. So even when the most popular client, geth, was taken out in an attack, the network stayed up by virtue of the nodes running other client implementations, e.g. Parity, or the C++ client, *eth*. Which was exactly as planned.

From the perspective of productivity, it has become obvious that for a developer, life could be made much simpler. There could be more support from the language and environment to assist in organizing the development and testing of larger systems. It would help in many ways if programs on Ethereum would perform closer to bare metal power.[51] Massive benefits could be expected from

50 Go is a modern programming language to develop large systems.

51 Running *on bare metal* means running a program as fast as possible, as close as possible to the processor hardware. There are often multiple layers separating a program from it. The virtual machine (see pg. 199) is one of them. Virtualization, as used in many cloud services,

more support with the challenges of consistency and the lack of guarantee for a transaction to actually reach the chain. Robustness would be boosted if we could re-use existing, thoroughly tested libraries, especially for crypto.

And in fact, all that is coming.

---

is another.

What is Ethereum Used for?

Many companies and hundreds of apps have been created or are being designed based on Ethereum. Some use the mainnet and some create their own, private Ethereum networks.

Programming a tailor-made digital currency on Ethereum is a special case. Most applications are way *more* complex than that.

The most powerful use cases are for the sharing economy, fintech, procurement[52] and Internet of Things (IoT).

Not too many projects are in production yet and the current limitations of Ethereum will have to be overcome for some business models to make sense. But this list illustrates the type of projects that Ethereum makes sense for.

Current development and officially presented concepts are for:

---

52 buying the goods and services that enable an organization to operate.

- Escrow services
- Smart NDAs

- Experimental governance
- Verifiable voting systems
- Community platforms
- Chats
- Microblogging
- Forums
- Password vaults
- Content curation

- P2P marketplaces
- General purpose *oracle*[53] services
- Prediction markets

- Ridesharing
- Social networks
- Dynamic health records
- Decentralized healthcare management
- Product origin tracking
- A carbon offset coin

- Advertising
- General job markets

- Retail insurances
- Retail futures

---

53 Oracle – see pg. 187.

- Crowd funding platforms
- Investment and lending platforms
- Micro lending
- Shares
- Financial derivatives trading
- Remittance services

- Identity systems
- Certification systems
- Reputation systems
- Know-your-customer (KYC) networks
- Ratings
- Employment credentials
- Price feeds
- Credit rating

- New currencies
- Cross chain trading
- Currency and equity exchanges
- Ether wallets
- Company building service
- Accounting
- Notary services
- Manufacturing support
- DAO automation
- Smart contract building

- Distributed file storage
- Distributed computation

- Name services and registrars
- Software audit repositories
- Software package managers
- Development build tools
- Frameworks for contract programming
- Network security

- A digital artwork registry
- Video and music streaming and distribution platforms
- Torrent catalogues

- Virtual worlds
- Games and lotteries
- Game items trade
- Gambling

- Art

Governance

Political fairness efforts and the sharing economy can reap great benefits:

- **Identity systems** are among the first projects being explored right now. At least two G7 countries are researching whether blockchains can help implementing electronic ids.

- **Voting** using the blockchain can be made tamper-proof and monitored using minimal effort.

- **Government** processes can be made transparent using the blockchain's audit-friendly features.

- **Titles** for land, a huge problem holding back the economy in developing countries, can be implemented in a transparent way.

- Collaborative models are being implemented that enable **direct democracy** and fair, contribution-based rewards.

While the auditability of a blockchain comes in really handy in these scenarios, the main feature is still the smart contract: that going forward, agreements will be kept exactly as promised in code.

For this to become really powerful one day, the development of an ecosystem will be required, where the contract code itself is screened and ok'ed by trusted, knowledgeable members of a society.

For titles, identity systems and access control, the blockchain adds an important element to electronic passports and licenses: it allows to revoke and modify them. A normal electronic license can only be made to expire after a certain time, much like a license printed on paper. Any attempt to revoke them requires a blacklist that has to be distributed to every single point where the license is checked.

If the license is a datapoint on the blockchain however, then it can be designed in a way so that it can be revoked by anyone who has the right key to do so. The change would only have to be transmitted to one node of the blockchain. The check points could get their information from any other node at their choosing. The license is highly available, not silo'ed and still modifiable. The trail of changes is auditable and cannot be fudged.

Fintech

Banks got excited about blockchain because their shareholders wondered if it's a threat or a savior. In some fields, banks may simply be replaced by a free and more effective service. But financial technology, as used by banks, will very likely also change, allowing banks to offer new services, powered by blockchains.

Specifically they will enable a safer implementation of main-stay products and might make tens of thousands of employees redundant who are now working to correct honest mistakes.

Most of all though, they could help to return transparency to the financial markets that has long been lost. And the key to that is a perplexing novelty:

Blockchains allow for *bearer-like,* yet perfectly *auditable* instruments.

Although it is taboo now in the financial world, bearer ownership makes risk transparent. The downside is usually that it is so hard to track. Blockchains bring the good part without the bad. To quote a metaphor from Pindar: *"when you let a bag of hundred dollar notes lie around, you know exactly what your risk is."* – that is the advantage of cash. And that is exactly what was missing in 2008 when the world financial system almost collapsed because banks stopped trusting each others completely, unable to decide who would survive to the next day. And rightly so because the banks themselves – except for Goldman Sachs and JP Morgan – could not figure what their *own* exposure was. A massive problem that persists today and some regulations only made it worse as some regulations force bank departments to *not* share information amongst each other, e.g. to avert insider trading.

What the financial system has now is a circuit breaker—type of security that augments systemic risks. Blockchains could help moderate the extremes by allowing for packet-ized, quantized models.

◆ Automation of **inter-banking markets** are a high hanging fruit, with smart contracts expressing the highly complex terms of products that today are defined by voluminous paper contracts. Synthetic CDOs with full access to their collateral might emerge so that a liquidity freeze like 2008 could not happen again: the market would resolve itself with contracts having full, automated access to their collateral, independent of market transparency, trust and liquidity of parties involved. *Blythe Masters* founded *Digital Asset Holdings* (DAH) to realize this vision.[54] DAH work on their own blockchain technology and also take part in the Linux Foundation's *Hyperledger* consortium, which works to create a blockchain suited for private fintech networks. However, a *public* network like Ethereum's is arguably best suited for a truly global, *interconnected* market of this kind.

◆ **Trade finance**, the origin of banking, could benefit massively from the transparency and pro-grammable custody, tied to a specific deliverable, that a blockchain solution for credit brings. Not only can banks verify and even enforce the claim of a smaller supplier against a dominating corpor-

---

54 Someone had a good laugh at me for believing this story. Anyway. It makes sense.

ation. Government can make sure regulations are respected and that for the benefit of the national economy, sub-contracting, smaller suppliers are being paid as agreed rather than squeezed by the government's main contractor. This is a major concern today e.g. in the DoD's dealings with Boeing.

◆ **Reporting regulations** might be transformed. The *Directorate-General Financial Stability, Financial Services and Capital Markets Union* (FISMA) of the European Commission[55] is exploring the first steps towards this in the context of ISA[2].[56] A feasibility study is conducted to find out if blockchain technology could be used to lower the burden of reporting for banks and make a quantum leap in the quality and speed of the resulting reports, to avert an 'information crisis' like 2008 to occur again. FISMA's vision requires 10,000 nodes and 10,000,000 transactions to be handled a day. Ethereum can't handle that workload now. But obviously, if this works one day, it will be a stepping stone for 'the real thing': going from reporting to have the actual contracts on the chain one day.

◆ Sending **remittances** basically for free instead of going through SWIFT is one retail example working today. This is arguably a Bitcoin use-case as this is about pure monetary transactions and the actual challenges lie in managing the outlets. Companies like Bitspark[57] or Abra[58] are in business for

---

55 The European Commission is the executive of the European Union.

56 ISA[2] – http://ec.europa.eu/isa/actions/isa2/03-access-to-data-data-sharing-open-data/15action_en.htm

57 Bitspark – https://bitspark.io

58 Abra – https://www.goabra.com

two years now with a technology based on Bitcoin. But R3's first tests included using Ethereum for settling remittances between banks and South Koreas *Hana* state their plans to use blockchain technology to reduce the cost of remittances.[59]

Bitcoin is too limited for more interesting applications and Ethereum might not remain the tool of choice, especially not for private chains. It is made for public networks, which is a much harder task and requires some hard trade-offs – e.g. for now, confidentiality – that banks by and large cannot make. But private chain–Ethereum variants like *Brainbot's*[60] *Hydrachain*[61] are being evaluated by big players.

A gargantuan task lies ahead to sit down and standardize existing paper contracts. Interestingly, regulatory requirements have prepared the ground here as they limited and formalized the variance of inter-banking contracts, to be able to better regulate them. This is what the European Commission's research is now building on.

Procurement

Procurement might end up completely re-invented.

◆ In procurement, 90% of work is in market research and negotiation of terms, which could all be automated by agents implemented as smart contracts. The focus here would be on standardizing offers and bids so that they can be articulated as smart contracts that define negotiation terms and agreements, covering fulfillment and payment.

---

59   Hana – http://www.hanafn.com/eng/pr/news/newsDetail.do?seq=3352

60   Brainbot Technologies – http://www.brainbot.com

61   Hydrachain – https://github.com/HydraChain/hydrachain

Again, as with law and fintech, it would be a fallacy to ignore the challenge that the transition from legal prose into program code poses. Procurement is even more free-wheeling than banking. This challenge is not solved at all just because we found a way to reliably execute coded contracts. An entire industry should spring up around this, with new types of computer-law and programming procurement specialists.

Internet of Things

The Internet of Things will enter a new era.

- ◆ Using the blockchain, machines can do business with each other (**M2M**); they can now have and spend their own budgets and optimize a household's spending. IBM and Samsung demonstrated that in early 2015 with their joint research project *ADEPT*[62] that was a demo of the influential *Device Democracy*[63] paper, spearheaded by Paul Brody.

- ◆ Machine-to-human interaction might be redefined by the emergence of **self-employed robot freelancers**. No kidding. Soon it's just the law in the way, not the technology anymore. Think of a self-driving car owning itself, unionized in the next form of Uber.

---

62 ADEPT – http://www.ibm.com/services/multimedia/ GBE03662USEN.pdf

63 Device Democracy – https://public.dhe.ibm.com/common/ssi/ ecm/gb/en/gbe03620usen/GBE03620USEN.PDF

♦ **Data analysis** can be pushed to the edge as IBM's *Blue Horizon*[64] demonstrates, allowing to use vast amounts of data that previously was just wasted and create a market where private contributors – 'citizen scientists' – are directly paid for the data they contribute. The *Weather Underground*[65] is an excellent example for the win-win mix of contribution and aggregation, as weather sensor data starts out *high volume, low value* and is condensed to *low volume, high value,* as far forward to the edge as possible. The vision for Blue Horizon is to enable start ups, with product ideas no one might have thought of as yet. Opening the path for them to a straight forward, scalable business model.

Plantoids

Now, now, Plantoids.[66] Beautiful steely sculptures of plants that perform a modest thank you gesture in light and movement when fed with bitcoins, happy that they were able to move closer to when they can reproduce.

Collecting money for being inspiring is their way to procreate: Once they collect enough bitcoins, they commission an artist to create a new plantoid in their image. With slight mutations as allowable with artistic license.

They are not owned by anyone but anchored in a DAO on the blockchain, programmed in Ethereum. There are three plantoids in existence these days, created by Primavera De Filippi. They are traveling the world and could be admired in Sydney and Paris at a COALA Block-

---

64 Blue Horizon – http://bluehorizon.network
65 Wheather Underground – https://www.wunderground.com
66 Plantoid – http://okhaos.com/plantoid/

chain Workshop and the Ouishare Fest. Last I heard, the big one is now hosted (not owned) by the Commonwealth Bank of Australia.

How To Create Your Own Digital Currency!

Ethereum was conceived as blockchain of blockchains: one that can do anything that any of the other blockchains could do, including Bitcoin, *Ripple*[67] or *Mastercoin*.[68]

And that's why, with Ethereum, everyone can create their own digital currency. That's right, you can have your own, you can make pre-sales and start being your own central bank.

The core of that invariably looks like this – just take in how brief the code is:

```
contract HelloCoin {
    mapping (address => uint) public balance;
    function mint(address receiver, uint amount) {
        balance[receiver] += amount;
    }
    function send(address receiver, uint amount) {
        balance[msg.sender] -= amount;
        balance[receiver] += amount;
    }
}
```

67 Ripple – https://ripple.com/
68 Mastercoin is now *Omni* – http://www.omnilayer.org/

Awesome or what? You can be rich in no time! The *only* thing that doesn't come bundled with Ethereum is that you have to convince people that your currency is actually worth anything.

But you could start modestly. Give away some trillions for free and try a modest initial exchange rate of a 1,000,000,000,000:1 on the dollar. It's money from thin air! It has been done! Someone should bite, it's how the world works. But at any rate you can pre-mine loads and become the richest person on Earth in terms of Hello-Coins. Gotta start somewhere.

Easy to ridicule, but this basic pattern might be the undoing of significant parts of the current fnancial industry and the healing of the world economy from much rent seeking.

Because blockchains are not about money from thin air. Remember, the reason they are so powerful, is that their scripts are executed on all computers of the network at the same time. The money from nothing was a genius way to crowd-fund the early systems and reward the people who dedicate server capacity to run nodes on. But from inception, it was really about peer to peer payments circumventing the banks.

Find a discussion of the code and notes on coding for a decentralized environment in the appendix, pg. 325.

How Does Ethereum Compare?

To add perspective, let's contrast Ethereum to household names, and newcomers.

Bitcoin

Both camps like to disagree but Ethereum is really an organic, logical evolution of Bitcoin. Ethereum was invented to allow for more interesting financial transactions than what Bitcoin could offer, and for an unlimited number of types of transactions, as opposed to Bitcoin's handful of standard transactions.

However, Ethereum quickly outgrew its original scope to become a bona fide platform to create automated commerce. For Bitcoin, there were some ill-fated attempts to build businesses around using smart contracts programmed in Bitcoin. While that confused a lot of people about the limitations of Bitcoin, they were always going to be horribly kludgy abuses of Bitcoin's capabilities.

What works is to take contract programming off-chain entirely (cfg pg. 37). This technique is often the common denominator whenever a chain-agnostic approach is pursued that is ideated to run on both Bitcoin and Ethereum, in the course giving up Ethereum's main improvements over Bitcoin.

Napster

There is a faint parallel between Ethereum and Napster, in that Ethereum is the opening shot for the disintermediation of entire industries. But Napster was pretty openly bent on enabling illegal activity, and while its payload was *distributed* across tens of thousands of computers, its file catalogue was *centralized*, so simply closing down its main servers was enough to put it out of business.

Ethereum is perfectly legal, will dis-intermediate middlemen across multiple industries and the technology is *decentralized,* there are no main servers.

BitTorrent

BitTorrent is a protocol for transferring files.

A main feature of files stored on BitTorrent networks is that they are practically impossible to take down – just like *smart contracts*.

Both BitTorrent and Ethereum are decentralized to be maximally resilient against attacks of any kind. It's simple – if you have no center, it's hard to take you out.

They are also both protocols rather than products or specific implementations. Which makes them even harder to stop: a protocol does not actually run, it's not a program, it's just a blueprint, an idea, a rule.

Otherwise, Ethereum and BitTorrent don't have too much in common, they are actually rather complementary: many Ethereum experiments in the past added BitTorrent to their Ethereum setup to transfer files, e.g. IBM's IoT projects ADEPT and Blue Horizon.

In the future, Ethereum will have *SWARM* and will be using *IPFS*[69] to ferry around block data – both share technical basics with BitTorrent.

Ripple and Stellar

Ethereum is more versatile, not focussed on finance, and a programming platform rather than an application.

Props to Ripple and *Stellar*[70] for doing what they did, basically starting out designing and implementing a blockchain from scratch, not aping Bitcoin. But they are intentionally more limited in use than Ethereum and, technologically, have since gone down different roads.

Ripple is breaking into the core banking world, trying to replace SWIFT for international transactions between banks. The break away team of Stellar cares more about helping the world by banking the unbanked.

Zcash

Zcash[71] is real. It is based on Bitcoin but offers total payment confidentiality. It's only logical as next evolution of Bitcoin, adds real hard math to solve a really hard problem and will likely trigger an escalation of cryptocurrency regulation. We'll see how that plays out.

While Zcash focusses on privacy in a way that Ethereum can't match, it otherwise has the same limitations as

---

69   The interplanetary file system – http://ipfs.io

70   Stellar – https://www.stellar.org

71   Zcash – https://z.cash. Previously known as ZeroCash, ZeroCoin.

Bitcoin and no smart contracts. This makes it a great complement to Ethereum and in fact Vitalik and Zcash's founder, *Zooko Wilcox*[72] are working on that together.

It's real competition in that, within days, it siphoned off almost half of Ethereum's miners when it was released at the end of October 2016. There was no ideological statement involved in that. But for a while, it simply paid better to mine Zcash rather than Ether.

Eris, Tendermint, Rootstock

Eris,[73] *Tendermint*[74] and *Rootstock*[75] started as forks of Ethereum, with individual special twists. A fork is when you take Open Source code and create your own thing from it that does not become part of the original project.

Eris and Tendermint add flexibility for other than public uses. Private chains (see pg. 194) have different needs than public ones, which latter Ethereum is made for. The private ones often need less defenses and more scalability.

Tendermint offers *proof–of–stake* (pg. 152) consensus, doing away with the bad electricity consumption inherent to *proof–of–work* (pg. 144), and implements better data consistency.

Eris is a platform for creating private and test chains, which are indispensable when you want to create a real system on Ethereum. No matter whether you intend to eventually run it on the public Ethereum mainnet, or on a private network. Developing on the Ethereum mainnet is

---

72 Zooko Wilcox – https://twitter.com/zooko
73 Eris – https://monax.io/platform
74 Tendermint – http://tendermint.com
75 Rootstock – http://www.rsk.co

simply too expensive and can be dangerous. Eris makes it easy to create, start and stop your own chains.

But Monax, the makers of Eris, are also aiming to make application development easier by providing contract libraries, called *engines*, and they claim that their *legal engineers* have most likely built the most complex smart contracts system to date for a fintech customer, who can't yet be named.

Eris features Tendermint as its native chain and tries to provide unified client interfaces across multiple chains – Ethereum, Tendermint, Bitcoin and Zcash. They also always had an eye on the topic of how to translate legal contracts into smart contracts.

They face a bit of a challenge in that they play catch up all the time with little support from the Ethereum guys. But so do the 'non-canonical' Ethereum clients and they all seem to be faring well.

Rootstock is joining Bitcoin with Ethereum for a very potent *sidechain* proposal. In effect, it's running the Ethereum virtual machine on Bitcoin mainnet instead of the Ethereum mainnet. So it deals in bitcoins rather than Ether but has full Ethereum–style smart contracts, written in Solidity.

It is attached to the Bitcoin mainnet by inviting miners to *merge-mine*: that is, mining for Bitcoin and Rootstock blocks simultaneously, without loss of Bitcoin hashing power. Their focus is to help banks with micropayments in Latin America. *Nick Szabo*, the inventor of *smart contracts*, said Rootstock joined the best of Bitcoin and Ethereum.

Eris, Tendermint and Rootstock are all firmly based on Ethereum and smart contracts will be programmed the same way, because they are re-using the part of Ethereum's

Open Source code that some say is 80% of what Ethereum *is:* the Ethereum Virtual Machine (EVM, see pg. 155).

And they are all, let's say, fringe cases with regard to style in Open Source, forking the effort mostly for their own benefit. The devs all know each other and were always cordial but it took an effort for some Ethereum people to embrace their new friends on the business side.

Parity

The brainchild of Gavin Wood, the author of Ethereum's *Yellow Paper,*[76] and former CTO of the Ethereum Foundation, the *Parity*[77] client is fully compatible with mainline Ethereum but will be in competition with it regarding protocol extensions. This means one can use Parity as normal Ethereum client, but one will also soon be able to create private networks with it that can do a bit more.

Scalability is high on Parity's agenda, and they position themselves as Ethereum variant of choice for private IoT networks. They hope to beat the *geth* team to the delivery of a production–ready, scaling Ethereum variant.

Dfinity

Created by Dominic Williams of *String Labs,*[78] backed by BCG Digital Ventures, Dfinity is supposed to become an Ethereum–like, public blockchain better suited for businesses. It features an innovative, scaling consensus algorithm (see pg. 142) that Dominic has worked on for

---

76 Ethereum Yellow Paper – http://gavwood.com/paper.pdf
77 Parity – https://ethcore.io/parity.html
78 String Labs – http://string.technology

two years and kept proposing to the core Ethereum guys. After it was not picked up he decided to go it alone in mid 2016.

Dfinity is to have a 'blockchain nervous system' that allows for majority decisions by stake holders e.g. about account freezing, to address catastrophic events like The DAO heist in a controlled fashion. While this looks like a professional necessity going forward, it could of course turn into an achilles' heel if it has the slightest flaw.

Dfinity also uses the EVM to execute smart contracts and accordingly their code will look just like Ethereum contracts. So if it is any good it doesn't seem unlikely that its consensus model will be picked up by Ethereum at some point to achieve scale.

Dfinity will be Open Source and have a test implementation running they say. But so far, technical information is hard to come by.[79]

Databases

Blockchains have successfully put many established wisdoms of database science on their head. There is no denying that. They are a successful new proposal for what data storage could look like. They focus on the angle how data can be made *trustable* and propose radical replication as answer.

> Blockchains add
> the dimension of *trust* to data.

---

79 Dfinity – http://dfinity.network

The trust we are talking about here is that *others* can trust what you store and do, and vice versa. It's not about securing your data on your node so that nobody else can change it, nor making sure that all your computations are 100% correct. Because if something goes wrong for you, the blockchain's solution is simply to kick you out of the network. It's up to you to safeguard your nodes and their data's integrity and find remedy if your node fails.

But integral to the mechanism of the blockchain is the power to determine whether your data is correct or not, to protect the *others* from you. And actually even you yourself.

> A blockchain protects the accounts when a node is compromised.

If someone highjacks your node, they still can't spend your cryptocurrency or change data you stored on the chain.[80] Because *your* data on your node is in no way a privileged copy over the thousand copies of your data on the other nodes. And accordingly, tampering with it does not alter your actual balance on the chain. The blockchain's consensus mechanism would detect it, cut your node out and stick with the majority opinion of all the other nodes about what your numbers should really be.

And this whole concept does not usually figure in database technology, which is focused on safeguarding your data on your side against the outside.

While in some way, a blockchain like Ethereum is really like a crazily, massively, many-times replicating database, its *cluster size* – *i.e.* the number of nodes that its

---

80 Except if you store your keys on the node, which you should not do.

network has – is *way bigger* than for any normal database, joining thousands of computers instead of dozens.

This requires different synchronization mechanisms between the computers that form the network. How to do that was a major invention that Bitcoin's creators brought to the table.

Neither Bitcoin nor Ethereum were designed with storage in mind first, as for example *Sia*[81] is, a decentralized, for–pay storage system for storing data 'at the edge', instead of in the cloud. Bitcoin and Ethereum just need to be able to store state somehow to be able to fulfill their function.

However, storing is not in itself that main function. But transacting digital currency in the case of Bitcoin, and executing smart contracts in the case of Ethereum.

Timestamping Services

Both Ethereum and Bitcoin can – and are – used as secure, auditable, public *storage of proofs of existence* for other data that resides out-of-chain.

There is a lot of really interesting stuff that can be done with just that technique. It's called *timestamping* (pg. 191) and it's a bit like how kidnappers send shots with their victim holding today's newspaper to proof that he or she is still alive. Just the reverse: such timestamp is a proof that something *already* existed at a given time.

But again that is not a database feature. It's something that can be added to any database, many vendors are actually doing that right now and some start calling themselves

---

81   https://sia.tech

blockchains or blockchain-enabled for it. Which is grossly misleading.

Internet

Ethereum can also be seen as Internet 3.0, the next step after social networks. In fact that ambition is why Ethereum's Javascript API was called *web3*.

Ethereum has the same architectural openness that allowed the Internet to grow so fast and become so versatile. Like the Internet, Ethereum is public, open source, decentralized and in essence actually a protocol, not any specific implementation. This is *not* necessarily true for many other tools on the Internet today, which became big successes by re-centralizing services:

Email used to go peer-to-peer, not across huge hubs like gmail et al. The glorious and unsung battle between web server systems that the Open Source community won with *Apache*, was fought so everyone could run their own web server for their own web pages. But instead, now everyone rents packages with a number of centralized providers and Internet access providers also didn't play along. Those web service packages would still be way more expensive though, if all the hosters had no alternative but to pay license fees to Microsoft instead of using the free Apache web servers.

Egan Ford, the lead architect of Blue Horizon, makes the point that what happened with the Internet, this re-centralization on top of a decentralized platform, will happen for blockchains, too. That we will see centralized hubs for specific services on top of the decentralized platform of a blockchain. Just like Facebook, Google and

Amazon established themselves with centralized services on top of the decentralized Internet.

Anyway, blockchains are in an early stage today, like the Internet was before the World Wide Web. Email and FTP existed quite some time before that. But at that point you hadn't seen the best part yet.

SkyNet

I told you it's a running gag. Seriously, SkyNet is the idea that mankind might construct a super computer that becomes sentient, can't be stopped, takes over and attacks mankind. Complete with time-traveling Terminator robots that try to change history.

We have very thoughtful people these days campaigning against autonomous killer robots at the UN. I was somewhat shocked to see the educated audience laugh about that at a recent blockchain panel. It hasn't really sunk in yet what's dawning upon us.

Of course, we have flying robots in service, with names ending on -or and spitting hellfire. Research to make them autonomous is on-going.

And there were ideas discussed about blockchain-based battle field communication at the first *Cryptoeconomicon* in early 2015. The interesting insider argument was that battle field commanders of the same side all don't trust each other with their information. If the military made any progress on that front, they won't tell us. It might have been an honest misunderstanding about what trust-less means.

But if, or rather when we get the first serious accidents involving robotic vigilantes, blockchain will be the least of our problems. The way that blockchains synchronize entities, in the abstract, looks more like a means to keep devices honest.

The SkyNet parallel is more in the notion of something man–made but unstoppable. As mentioned, Bitcoin and Ethereum have this awesome *high availability* feature that if only one node survives, they always come back up and restart the entire network. In this context it is a bit scary. It should at least give us pause. In the Terminator movie though, SkyNet is removed from human access by residing on satellites in orbit.

And what do you know, we do have serious efforts under way to launch satellites running Bitcoin nodes, so no state player can ever cut out the last Bitcoin miner! This might be an appealing idea for the Ethereum community, too. In both communities, there are lots of really interesting characters with a lot of money at their hands now. A BitSat satellite is said to come for as low as $1M. With a market cap of $1B the Ethereum community should be able to find that money.

Now SkyNet is all about AI starting to make decisions that it were not meant to make. And as mentioned before, the characteristics of untold numbers of smart contracts acting in concert are highly unpredictable. They will not get sentient. But each one will be imbued with some modest form of 'intelligence', statistical algorithms and optimizations.

What kind of behavior they will show in concert, is anybody's guess. Their oscillations will likely 'only' ever crash economies. The side effects of this might very soon affect human beings though. In a merciless, de-humanized way and without direct recourse.

Now the fun bit is the time travel part. Changing history is a big topic in the Ethereum world, at least since The

DAO *hard–fork* (see pg. 286). For good or bad, you can in fact have a huge impact by retroactively changing the rules of the game. If Ethereum was ever to take over, it's exactly how it would be stopped: with a system code change that would surgically take out whatever went wrong. Even in the past. That is, if everyone running nodes can agree.

Otherwise, you'll see a SkyNet and a SkyNet Classic duking it out across parallel universes.

Colossus

Meanwhile in the real world, chances are that regulators might take blockchain tech out before it even gets started and push it into illegality. It will of course still work, technically, just like BitTorrent.

But another question altogether is, what might happen if governments seize on blockchains big time, decree that they must always follow certain transparency rules and find the perfect tool of control in it?

To that point: before SkyNet, there were *Colossus*[82] and *Guardian!* Another classic movie, two super computers, made invincible and put in charge of the US and USSR nuclear arsenals respectively. They were allowed to connect and sync and of course they decided to take over the world to protect us from ourselves, killing one of their creators while putting the other under close observation 24/7. He then manages to wrestle bed room privacy from his digital Frankenstein monster.

According to Huxley, an Ethereum Colossus would of course reign softly, using electronic money rather than directing armed forces. That's much more powerful, less confrontational and visible. We can then discuss for ages

---

82   Colossus – the Forbin project, 1970.

when the exact moment of no return from 'benevolent' machine tyranny was. With the autonomous killer drone technology becoming available, as well as the existing elaborate apparatus of surveillance, all elements are in place for the machines to protect us really well.

For something nightmarish like this to happen, all that's needed are good intentions. Maybe some things will appear rather spontaneously, emerging along the lines of the meta logic of game theory.

We managed to allow for Giant Vampire Squids to emerge that are too big, or just too well connected to fail. We might be well on our way to create a new, more agile form of a self sustaining, anonymous power structure.

But you can program your own cryptocurrency to fund the resistance (goto pg. 70)!

How Does Ethereum Work?

Ethereum has myriads of accounts as its global state.

An account consists of an account number and a balance. And someone has the secret key to make transactions from it. It can also have code associated that is executed automatically whenever it receives a payment. Many accounts exist for the sake of their code and are created and called like functions in a program library.

The code can have *static state*, i.e. variables that survive individual calls to the account's code, which is the main invention of Ethereum over Bitcoin. A prime example is the account's balance itself, which Bitcoin also does *not* have. But the state can also include lists and small strings. Accounts therefore look somewhat like object instances of object oriented languages, grouping together state and code that operates on it.

An account can be

♦ an *externally operated account* (EOA),
   i.e. manually controlled via its secret key and
   usually existing for its balance, or

♦ a *contract*,
   existing mostly for its code and state.

Technically, this distinction will go away in future versions of Ethereum. But regardless, the above highlights the two different uses an address, or account, can have in Ethereum.

What is special about the Ethereum accounts is that, as mentioned before, their contents is stored on *every* full Ethereum node, mirrored thousands of times around the globe.

And that when its balance changes, it changes on all these thousands of nodes at the same time. No other database technology does that. It is actually pretty unhinged. But it makes the whole thing work.

The Ethereum network per se is lifeless.

For anything to happen in the network, someone has to sign off on something that is then causing ripple effects through the network to get resolved.

The order of things is:

1. user input into an EOA triggers a compute cycle;

2. messages from EOA trigger contracts to execute;

3. contracts can call other contracts;

4. the network computes until all calls originating from the first transaction are resolved.

So if you can't help but have to think of a blockchain as a database, then this can be thought of as database triggers firing off after a state change. That's nothing new obviously.

But again, the innovation is that this happens simultaneously on all nodes of the network and can't be stopped. Plus, that anything going in must be digitally signed by an account holder.

Which is nothing like a database. It's a blockchain.

BLOCKCHAIN

"a solution to the double-spending problem
using a peer-to-peer distributed
timestamp server
to generate computational proof
of the chronological order of transactions."

Satoshi Nakamoto

What is a Blockchain?

Hang on. It's not actually *that* hard to understand, neither deep crypto nor math. It's a bit of a social game.

It might be futile at this point in time to try a definition of the term *blockchain* that everyone can agree with. The chance at a useful definition might be over since marketing people found that it sells. Virtually all big brands publish articles these days that are just not fully correct or intentional fud. The damage the *distributed ledger* meme does is immense.

But everyone means *something* when they say 'blockchain', charting out the competing notions reveals how tangled perceptions are.

After reviewing that we will go deeper and look at the individual moving parts that a blockchain consists of. That is, before you can invent your own definition. Seriously.

Practical Rules of Triangulation.

Let's take a step back. You will frequently have to figure out in a polite way what a business partner or author might mean when they use the word. Here is a laundry list of the most common perceptions. Note how some read as if they were opposites of each other.

A blockchain is understood as something that

♦ helps make data 100% *trustworthy*

♦ facilitates *trust-less* interaction

♦ forces data to be *freely accessible / visible*

♦ allows to *anonymously* buy drugs online

♦ leaves *traces* for every transaction

♦ can be used to manage identities

♦ prevents *honest errors*

♦ prevents errors from *being fixed*

♦ prevents anyone from *changing* data ex-post

♦ empowers miners[83] to *change history*

♦ can *prove* a certain state at a given time

♦ cannot guarantee for data to *ever* be *final*

♦ creates *money from nothing*

♦ can be used to *mirror* real assets

♦ will make banks *obsolete*

♦ could be a *productivity boost* for banks

♦ will end hyper capitalism

♦ hastens the *commodification* of everything

♦ will empower the developing world

♦ will help to bank the unbanked

♦ helps *evading* taxes and launder money

---

83 Miners – see pg. 134

- can help to *end* tax-evasion and money laundering
- is all about *distribution*
- is stuck with a *singleton* model
- is all about *decentralization*
- is the ultimate *centralization* of perspective

All of the above is somewhat correct, including the apparent contradictions. Some of it will change. Some points are a distraction from what the actual value is. And those sideshows prepare the stage for 'competitors' to come in that focus on just that aspect and do it, literally, around a million times better. Be it real databases, legacy payment systems or contract law.

Technically, a blockchain is usually associated with

- transaction data
- digital assets
- cryptography

It is often thought of as a hog of data, the word sounds somewhat like a static thing. Blocks and all. And in fact blockchains have an obesity problem.

Mainnet and Stack.

Frequently, the entire software system is called the 'blockchain'. In that case it means the concrete tech itself – e.g. the Bitcoin or Ethereum client software. *And* a live, global network of computers, too, that drives and hosts that data.

The Bitcoin and Ethereum *mainnets* themselves are called 'blockchains.' And although it is easy to take the Ethereum source code – it's freely available – and start up a new chain that works exactly like Ethereum, many people would not readily agree that your new chain is a 'real blockchain.' Even though technically it certainly is.

At any rate, after various hard–forks, Ethereum theoretically has eight mainnets or more now. Even if only two – Ethereum and Ethereum Classic – are listed at the *exchanges*.[84]

A blockchain is *decentralized*: mirrored thousands of times.

It's not a blockchain if its copies are not stored, identically, across massively many computers.

Keeping all those blockchain copies in sync is done using a *consensus protocol*.

The special protocol invented for Bitcoin that can keep thousands of computers in sync uses proof–of–work (pg. 144). Ethereum uses an improved version of it, called *GHOST*, which is much faster.

A blockchain *has* a transaction ledger.

Fundamentally, the data a blockchain holds is a *sequence of transactions*. And as of today it is essential that no transaction is ever forgotten.

The blocks do not necessarily consist of *state* information, as in

account A has 42 coins

---

84   Exchanges buy and sell cryptocurrencies for real world money.

but, instead, of *transactions* of the form

account X transfers 42 coins to account A.

This holds true especially for Bitcoin. In case account *A* was only ever involved in one transaction, then the second statement expresses the same as the first, plus a little more: A now has 42 coins (and they came from X).

If there are more statements, the balance is the sum of them:

account X transfers 42 coins to account A;

account A transfers 23 coins to account Y,

this implies:

account A has 19 coins.

which latter, again, is not stored on the Bitcoin blockchain. Just the transfers are. And obviously, to understand the balance e.g. of account X, one would have to make sure that one knows all the transactions ever made using X.

Ethereum goes one step further and includes both state and transactions in its blocks. This will help scaling Ethereum. Because in the end, you want to know the current balance, A=19, and not all the transactions leading up to it, which can be very many.

So Bitcoin transactions simply transfer bitcoins between accounts. I send one bitcoin from my account to your account. That's it.

Technically, the transaction consists of:

- ◆ a sender account number
- ◆ a receiver account number and
- ◆ an amount.

There is more to it because of fees and a required internal mechanism to give change.

While an Ethereum transaction can be much more complex than that, in its simplest form, it is exactly like this. Just what I send would be *Ether*, instead of bitcoin.

Now, typically, data is only ever added to a blockchain and never removed. That results in some nice properties. And a database doing this is called a 'ledger'.

But for blockchains this is really more like a technical artifact that poses a big scalability obstacle and might change in the future. The Cypherpunk inventors of Bitcoin will doubtlessly have seen it as a disadvantage.

So use cases that are based on a blockchain functioning like a ledger, somehow place their faith into a side effect that holds blockchain technology back.

Blockchains *might* soon not have ledgers anymore.

Interestingly though, even when Ethereum one day progresses to a version that sheds old data – like the Parity client already does – you will still get the same *guarantees* out of it that people appreciate about ledgers.

It will be a bit of a tougher sale, because the actual transaction data might be gone but the *proof* that the transaction was made will still be there. This might be good enough for a lot of business cases where it is not interesting what was before, just that what is inspected was not conjured up.

Still, Parity also shows how the entire historical block data can still be available, on–demand. So blockchains might someday feature a type of hyper–scalable, sharded ledger that always has all old data stored somewhere, available when needed for an audit.

However, the ledger is but one part of it, where the chain stores transactions to. And it's a problematic part as right now, it just keeps growing and making it grow faster has even become an attack vector on Ethereum.

A blockchain could be described as a new type of database with 'magic' stored procedures.

In the database analogy, the more complex transactions of a blockchain can be compared to a database's *stored procedures* and *triggers*.

Especially the Bitcoin blockchain is in nature close to the underbelly of a modern database system. Those also use *sequences of transactions* as their underlying representation of data, rather than state: the rows and columns a SQL RDBMS[85] shows you are usually but an abstraction that makes it easier for humans to use and reason about the data. But this is not how the data is stored underneath. The actual data stored are the *inserts*, *updates* and *deletes* you issued. Expressing data this way makes it easier to pull consistent *backups* and to *distribute* the data across multiple machines in a server cluster.

---

85 Relational Database Management System, since decades the standard flavor of business databases. E.g. ORACLE and MySQL.

A Bitcoin *wallet*[86] shows the same kind of abstraction when it shows the balance of your Bitcoin addresses. This balance does not exist anywhere on the Bitcoin blockchain. What exists are only the transactions into and out of an address, which will result into this balance if you add them all up from block #1. The wallet calculates that result.

Mathematically this is quite elegant. It sucks a bit in practice because it doesn't *scale* very well. This means that the system as it is, will never be able to do much more than around 10 or maybe one day 100 transactions per second.

This is why the approach was changed for Ethereum. Ethereum does all that and then it *also* stores the balance of every account.

The rationale for doing it this way was to make the system simpler. Whether that really worked as expected might be debatable. Because on the implementation side, the actual requirements to have a robust and performant system eventually result into the need to have something like those insert, update and delete logs running under- neath at any rate.

But meanwhile, an Ethereum wallet shows account balances that *actually exist* on the Ethereum blockchain as a datapoint.

Yet, as of today, Ethereum still shares with Bitcoin that at any time, any balance can be calculated from the trans- actions stored in the chain alone, calculating all of them through from the first, the genesis block.

So the state is somewhat redundant in Ethereum cur- rently. But this makes it easier to discard old transactions,

---

86 A wallet is a program one uses to manage one's bitcoins or Ether. If you buy things using cryptocurrency, it is usually by making a trans- fer from one of your accounts to somebody else's account, with the help of your wallet program.

to *garbage collect* the world state, as the Parity client does. Which speeds some things up markedly and saves a lot of disk space. And having explicit state helps with the creation of a *sharded network* to achieve better scalability.

A blockchain uses other database systems.

In the end, the blockchain data has to be persisted to disk somehow, i.e. stored on some computer. Oftentimes, it is stored on hard disk using a slim key-value database, e.g. Google's *LevelDB*. That's what the Go Ethereum client does.

So while a blockchain can itself be seen as a new type of database, it uses established database technology behind the scenes, on the lower level, to write its data to disk.

This is unsurprising, other successful, new *distributed databases* do the same: when it's time to actually write to disk, there is no need to reinvent the wheel.

For most of the new distributed databases that came up through the last decade, the magic is in how the computers of a network cluster play together, not how to write things to disk. Same for blockchains.

There is another similarity: the new breed of distributed databases, inspired by Amazon's *Dynamo* paper,[87] often share the weak consistency guarantees (pg. 124) of blockchains. At least the blockchains we see today. Almost all Ethereum research today favors stronger consistency.

---

87 Dynamo – http://www.allthingsdistributed.com/files/amazon-dynamo-sosp2007.pdf

A public blockchain is open to anyone.

By design, the Bitcoin and Ethereum mainnets are open for anyone to join as a miner or transactor. You can start a client and run it as a miner in minutes. You can create an account for Ethereum or Bitcoin and start receiving money immediately. It's supposed to be like that.

If you run a regular client, even if you don't mine, the first thing it does is downloading the entire blockchain data since the genesis block.

All that data is needed to verify what the current state should be. But it also contains all transaction data of everyone who ever made a transaction. It's all on your hard disk then. And it's like that for everyone else in the network, too.

Light clients help scaling.

Both Ethereum and Bitcoin also have *light clients*. Ethereum's is still in beta. Light clients do what clients actually, originally were not supposed to do in a blockchain, they trust other nodes to some extent and don't go all the way to verify all blocks from genesis when coming into the network, nor check every new block for validity. They do some tests, but in the end, they need a full client that co-operates with them to work.

Ethereum's light client does much less work than a full client, loads less data and trusts a regular client to supply it with the truth on-demand: reliable bits of the world state of the network that all the full clients are in consensus about.

Light clients are important for many applications but the networks could not consist solely of those. Someone has to take care of the validation work.

A blockchain uses cryptography.

But actually not that much. Most importantly, there is *no encryption* taking place to encrypt the data on the blockchain, quite to the contrary. It's all in the open. Just the traffic between nodes is encrypted. But if you become a node yourself, which anyone can, you can see everything.

The two elements that are used throughout are *hashes* and *digital signatures*. Let's look at that.

What is Cryptography?

The art of writing and solving codes.

Which in practice means techniques for secure communication.

In the context of blockchains though it is more about making sure

1. *who* sends a transaction and that

2. the *past* can't be tampered with.

Cryptography's potential for use for espionage and cyber attacks has led many governments to classify it as a weapon or to prohibit its use and export. At one point you couldn't even download and use the original Netscape Navigator[88] in Europe because it contained encryption that was export–restricted by the U.S.

These days, encrypted mobile phone data of deceased terrorists makes for a new round of controversies. But it's more about getting at the keys now or building back doors in. The cryptographic math itself is considered to be out of the barn. At least the parts we know about.

---

88   Netscape was the 90's web browser.

Big numbers and random.

Cryptography uses the mathematical peculiarities of very big numbers, primes, calculus and randomness.

For example, while it is a fast operation to take large numbers and multiply them, it is *not* fast to do prime factorization of big numbers.

These kind of functions are called *trap-door*, because while it's easy to go one way, you can (almost) not get back to where you came from.

> ## Crypto is
> *trap-door math.*

For crypto purposes, one person uses the one direction and then the point is that no one can easily get back to the starting point, even if they are told what the endpoint was. They *could* but it would take forever. Unless, of course, they had a quantum computer.

Digital signatures.

This reflects how digital signatures work. You need special knowledge – the *private key* – to create a signature and you have to keep that knowledge – this key – secret so that no one can forge your signature.

> ## A digital signature
> ## uses a secret key.

The creation of that key takes a bit of time. And back in the day, it actually really involved juggling very large, randomly picked primes.

When you digitally sign something, the algorithms involved make it easy to check for others that the signature was really made by you. But virtually impossible for others to create such signature, without knowing your random choices.

In the simplest cases, what happens in these calculations – the key creation, signing and check of the signature – is essentially random prime number generation, multiplication and division with one side using primes the other side doesn't know which they are.

Blockchains use different type keys that are based on how hard it is to guess the formula for a complex graph when only knowing a few points on it. But the purpose of the math is the same, to create a good trap-door.

Public-private key pairs.

The procedure actually needs a second key, called the *public key*. This key is created at the same time that the secret, private key is created. They work their magic only with each other.

Which is that something encrypted with the one can be decrypted with the other. The public key is made public, for anyone to use and the private key must be kept secret.

This has two applications:

the public key can be used to encrypt something, anything and only the private key can decrypt it. This is how secret messages can be sent, albeit in one direction.

The private key can be used to encrypt something and the public key can be used to decrypt it to prove that it could only have been encrypted by its corresponding private key. This is a digital signature and how it is verified.

> A digital signature
> also needs a 'public key'.

Digital signatures are not for encryption.

Signatures are *based on* encryption and use secrets to work but they are *not* per se used to hide anything. They do not encrypt what is being signed. The signature is a separate thing, a small file, some unreadable bytes.

You usually bundle up the signed data with the signature. Because for people to check if the signature is valid *for this data* – like set to that specific document – they need to see the data and make a calculation based on it.

But the most 'crypto' that Bitcoin and Ethereum use are signatures, not actual encryption. The stuff in their chains is *not* currently encrypted. It would be nice if it were but for the way Bitcoin and Ethereum work, it's a challenge.

> Bitcoin and Ethereum are
> not encrypted. Yet.

Zcash however, is fully encrypted and leads the way in this area.

Hashes.

Hash algorithms do something weird, they project the infinite on a limited set of numbers that is still large enough to be *practically* infinite.

This is used in a very pragmatic fashion: because the numbers *are* finite, they can be written down and are not actually that long. Because there are *practically* infinitely many, they can be used as universally unique IDs that will never run out.

A hash is somewhat like a cross sum,[89] just better. Like with a cross sum, a hash formula takes every single digit, letters too, of whatever you are *hashing* and calculates a result from that, the hash.

But a hash formula doesn't only add everything up, it also multiplies, throws in factors and summands, in seemingly chaotic fashion. Letters, of course, on this level are treated like numbers. E.g. 'a' is 65 etc.

A hash formula is really complex. And it's even important in the context of blockchains that it takes a little bit of time to calculate it, but not too much.

Like with a cross sum, the result – the hash – is much shorter than the original data that is being hashed.

And one cannot get back to the original data from the hash. It's a one-way street.

There are different hash algorithms. One hash algorithm that was once popular was called *MD5*. For example, this text:

MD5's designer Ron Rivest has stated "md5 and sha1 are both clearly broken (in terms of collision-resistance)". So

---

89 The cross sum is the sum of a number's digits, repeatedly applied. E.g. the cross sum of 1373 is 5 because 1+3+7+3 = 14 => 1+4 = 5.

MD5 should be avoided when creating new protocols, or implementing protocols with better options. SHA256 and SHA512 are better options as they have been more resilient to attacks (as of 2009).

has the MD5 hash:

ed7f56281b8d079ff101009105f75b44

And because MD5 is broken, Bitcoin and Ethereum are using another algorithm, called *SHA-256*. Which is considered not broken until the opposite is shown.

Hashes are used as if they were unique identifiers.

The hash *ed7f56281b8d079ff101009105f75b44* can be used as a unique *id* for the above text, for two reasons:

1. If any punctuation or word was changed, you'd get a different hash for it.

2. You will not for your life be able to find another text that results into exactly this hash.

So our hash does not only id this text, but really the exact version of this text. Any minuscule change to it and you get a new hash that can serve as id for that new version.

Now, a hash calculation routinely crunches through megabytes of data to return a hash of just 16 or 32 bytes size. That 'every data input results into a different hash' is *not* literally true *at all* but that's the 'magical' part:

Even if you have gigabytes or terabytes of data as input, if you change only a single bit, you will end up with a different hash for it.

So for example, if you just leave away the last dot of that paragraph about MD5's brokenness above, you'll end up with the hash

e7cd6cc5b1450aa7abb4ebda87c99fce

instead.

And importantly, there is basically no way anyone could tell that our previous hash and this new one have anything to do with each other.

And no way to guess the text that they were created from, or that the texts that were the input for the two hashes were almost exactly the same.

Hashes are the links of Cypherspace.

Cypherspace can be imagined as the space of all texts and numbers that could possibly exist. This goes beyond cyberspace, where everything is addressable with an IP number, or a URL. Cypherspace holds not only what exists but all that could.

And with a hash you have a useful id of anything in Cypherspace that kind of points backwards: you will know that it's the right id when you see what it points to, the original text. This id does not help you to find the text. And that's a feature. But once you see the text later, you have proof that someone meant *that* text and no other when they gave you the id. In crypto, that is very useful.

Good hash algorithms have no *collisions*.

It is not true that hashes are unique – i.e. that no other text could result into the same hash – but pretending they are is very useful. It's so not true: there really is, for every hash, an *infinite number* of texts that will all result into the *same hash*. But you won't find any. If you did, it was called a *hash collision*.

Also, theoretically one should be able to find out how to cleverly change some bytes in some text so that one ends up with the same hash as before! This would break digital signatures. And the possibility exists. But it's just totally unlikely.

However, this is exactly what researchers look for to find out if a hashing algorithm is any good.

Those collisions are ridiculously hard to find. There is not really a formula for that, it's a lot of trial and error. Like rolling stories with letter dices. Sure, they are all in there. But it'll take forever to find just one that makes any sense.

So for all *practical* intents and purposes:

> Two different data sets will 'always' result into two different hashes.

And blockchains *completely* rely on that.

Hashes are even considered to be *quantum-proof*. Meaning, not even the advantages of quantum computers are expected to break them by finding useful collisions.

On the other hand, after a while, researchers *did* find ways to create collisions for *MD5* and *SHA-1*.

Which is why they are not used anymore even though for some time they had been considered safe.

Trusting that a quattuorvigintillion ids will suffice.

The 32 bytes of a hash reflect a number between zero and one hundred quattuorvigintillions. Sure, that's a lot less than there are atoms in the universe, you say, but still a lot. A one with 77 zeros. That's roughly how many different hashes there are.

And that's why, if the hash algorithm is good, then it is just incredibly unlikely you'll ever end up with the same hash, no matter how many different inputs you try.

So what are the hash formulas?

Many different algorithms exist to create hashes. They have names like *MD5*, *Keccak*, *SHA-1* or *SHA-256*. Hashes are so important for CS, business and defense that the US National Institute of Standards and Technology (NIST) held an open competition in 2009 to find the best possible algorithm.

Bitcoin and Ethereum both use an older one, devised by the NSA in 2001, called *SHA-256*. It gives 32-byte long resulting hashes, as opposed to the 16 bytes of MD5. Which obviously reduces the chances for collisions. The USA has a patent on SHA-256, *#6829355*, but they extend a royalty-free license.

The most important part is of course, that you can trust that your hash formula does not have a back–door where someone in the know, say the inventor, knows how to find collisions. They could break your system for good.

Especially if the system has no concept of collisions at all and just assumes they can't happen.

Bitcoin and Ethereum trust the NSA with that.[90]

And the fun fact remains that a hash collision could be found at any time and no-one knows how the Bitcoin or Ethereum blockchains would react when they would run into one.

It's really not that likely though.

---

90 Bitcoin's makers were a bit more wary and mixed RIPEMD-160 in.

What's the Magic?

Decentralization, signatures, hashes.

Ready to roll? The basic potions are as just discussed:

- *decentralization* for the execution guarantee:
  so agreements become unstoppable programs.

- *signatures* as mandatory authorization:
  so every single bit on the blockchain is signed.

- *hashes* as proofs for the entire world state:
  so agreeing on 32 bytes means agreeing on all.

If you blend these ingredients and let the result dry you get the fairy dust of cryptocurrency and, most of all, self executing contracts. Let's see how.

Valuable numbers.

In a way what came true is a Cypherpunk wet dream: numbers that carry value.

> ### Keys are secret numbers that work like cash.

For a blockchain you can claim that your secret key, which is but a long column of digits, *is* such a number.

It's not a fixed value. It depends on what is stored to the blockchain account it controls. So the number is really just charged up, not valuable per se. The value is not fiat, just cryptocurrency. But effectively, this key carries that value, anyone who knows this number, possesses the value. Like cash.

Decentralization provides for the *guarantee of execution*.

The 'magic' of decentralization starts with how copying everything to everybody lays the ground to pre-empt copying. In the case of cryptocurrency, preventing the duplication of coins.

Because everyone has all the data, everybody can check the validity of every single change in the world state, and so therefore, nobody can cheat and pretend something that is not true. E.g. that a certain account has x coins on it while it really just had y. Everybody else would immediately catch it.

The same holds for more complex transactions or sizable programs – Ethereum's *contracts* – that run on the chain. Every node checks every contract's result.

Total validation
replaces central control.

This total validation mechanism obsoletes the need for a privileged master node. All nodes are *effectively* equal.

And thanks to that, equally dispensable.

This equality of the nodes then is the foundation for the unstoppable[*] programs on the blockchain, the *smart contracts*: because all logic is run by all nodes the exact same way, it doesn't matter if some nodes crash and some make honest or dishonest mistakes. The program will complete on *some* nodes and that is enough.

If the program is an agreement between two parties, no tricks will allow any party to cancel the contract or to not fulfill their part. Some nodes will run it. The agreement will be executed. And then money will be sent left or right.

> Cryptocurrency empowers smart contracts.

For smart contracts to really make sense, they have to have the ability to effect a value transfer. That can be done in different ways but cryptocurrency, or digital assets, is the only perfect one that is as unstoppable as the contract itself. Everything else makes the contract as weak as the weakest link in its payment chain.

---

[*]   except if you manage to persuade thousands of people to alter their nodes.

Cryptocurrency payment is a smart contract.

Now we go full circle: cryptocurrency is enabled in the exact same way that smart contracts are, which are just a more general case. Every cryptocurrency transfer is but a simple smart contract. The mechanism is one and the same, it's just a smart contract's simplest form: one signature and the money moves.

In fact, Ethereum's smart contracts grew out of the transactions of Bitcoin that are implemented as small scripts. No surprise they are at their best when dealing in cryptocurrency.

And to answer this question right here, for the input side, the blockchain can certainly not 'see' nor enforce anything in the real world. But how to get information from the real world into the smart contract is part of its setup. That's exactly what the role of an *oracle* is (see pg. 187).

Digital signatures enable trust-lessness.

For blockchains, the signatures are important to make sure that *new transactions do indeed come from the person authorized to issue them*, a key element in the mechanics of smart contracts. In fact:

> ### Knowing its private key
> ### means *possessing* the account.

Now, if you stole the key, you still don't legally own the cryptocurrency stored in the account. But you control it.

The blockchain is agnostic about the difference between ownership and possession. As far as the blockchain is concerned:

The key is
the authorization.

Because it is certain that who opened the account had the key and every signature for every transaction out of it has to be signed with this key.

If you have the key you can initiate a transaction. If you don't you don't. Again a bearer–like feature. If you give the key to somebody else that's all you need to do to authorize them, from the blockchain's point of view.

And it cuts both ways. If a transaction was made it was done by someone who holds the key. If you used that key for other stuff that identifies you, it can be concluded that the transaction was probably made by you.

There is no repudiation of signatures that you make with a key, as far as the blockchain is concerned.

But the picture is different in the real world. Of course you could have shared the key or someone could have stolen it. So it is less straight forward to link the key to a person.

Key ownership
can be repudiated.

Everything on a blockchain is digitally signed.

Code is deployed to the blockchain in Ethereum as payload of a transaction and thus, is also signed.

This gives blockchain data the unique feature that all its permutations are signed off. All input and all code is signed, and so, by extension, the result.

The important point is how blockchains are based on this primitive of authorization – your signature – as the central building block of everything a blockchain consists of. As noted before:

> Because everything is signed,
> there is no need to trust.

The account numbers are derived from the public keys.

Notably, there is no act of creating an account in the Bitcoin or Ethereum blockchain. You just create your private-public key pair – with your preferred tool, you don't interact with the blockchain for that – and you have an account.

One could say:

> All accounts 'pre-exist.'
> You just grab a random key for one.

You can tell the account number to other people, and they can send money to it, all without you ever touching the chain.

The account number – or 'address' – follows directly from the public key that you created. It's basically just a hash of the public key.

So every account has only one private key.

And which account number you get is completely random, decided during the moment that you create your key pair.

Theoretically somebody else could come up with the same private and public keys and thus with access to your account. It's just not likely.

This looks like skipping a confirmation step that one would expect with a serious thing like an account creation. And that's true. It's missing. Using very big numbers and good randomness allows for an elegant leap over that.

The main blockchain crypto magic is the hash.

Now we get down to the clockwork.

Developers are so used to hashes, we don't think of them as magic anymore. The first crypto–related thing that comes to mind when thinking of blockchains are *private-public keypairs*, not hashes.

But the hash is more central to it.

Most prominently, what is hashed in a blockchain are the *blocks*, which contain the transactions. A hash, called the *blockhash*, is calculated from this data. Hashes are used in multiple places but this is the most relevant one.

The important part is that *you get the same hash if, and only if, you have the same transactions in the block, in the same order.*

The blockhash fixes *which* transactions, in *what order.*

A blockchain is a tamper-proof way to store a sequence of transactions.

So the blockchain data consists of blocks, which (mainly) consist of transactions.

The transactions within a block are ordered.

The blocks are in a specific order, too.

There is a first block, called *genesis block*.

And each following block contains a hash of the previous block.

The hash of the last block, therefore, contains hashed hashes of all previous blocks.

The nested chain of blockhashes, is the 'chain' in 'blockchains.'

So each hash is hashed again with the complete data of the next block, to get that next block's blockhash. Obviously, this means that each blockhash is depending on the previous blockhash and if one previous block was different – i.e. had different transactions or the transactions in a different order – then all blockhashes after that block would be different, too, as one different hash would ripple through the entire chain coming after it.

This makes it nearly impossible to tamper with past transactions that get ever deeper buried under new blocks.

> ## Past transactions become the harder to revert the older they are.

You'd have to unpack and rehash all blocks that came after the block that it's in and you end up with different blockhashes all the way. The tell tale sign that something was touched up.

And intentionally, the considerable time it takes to satisfy the proof–of–work conditions for consensus for each block, makes it technically almost impossible to calculate fast enough to come up with an 'alternate reality' for a blockchain. Effectively, one has to win a race against the united calculation power of all the nodes in the chain.

Nodes agree on only one hash.

Now, if two parties independently replay all the transactions and *arrive at the same last hash* for their last block, they can be sure that *every single transaction they executed before was the same*.

This one small data point of 32 bytes, this one hash at the end, ensures that they look at the exact same set of transactions the whole way. All they have to do is to compare one hash to know that their inputs as well as their results are the same.

Concretely, we are talking about gigabytes of data for both Ethereum and Bitcoin. Even with millions of transactions, looking at one hash is enough.

This is relevant because of how hard it is for two or more computers to be sure that they look at the same data. Being able to focus on only 32 bytes and find agreement about that makes the whole task of finding *consensus* a lot easier.

Accordingly, this last hash is used to find consensus between all nodes about the entire world state of the system. Based on *independent calculation of all transactions* by every single node.

A blockchain guarantees *correct future state*.

Now, if, going forward, those two parties

1. only accept transactions digitally *signed* by the owner of whatever it is that is transacted, and

2. can agree on the *order* of new transactions,

then they can be certain to stay in sync in regard to the world state, in all eternity.

Which is exactly the procedure all nodes follow from the very first block.

The ways to corrupt the chain are limited.

The only way to disrupt the nodes' lockstep would be to withhold information that one side has to receive from the other, e.g. cut their connection.

But because of the requirement that transactions need to be signed, the world state *cannot* be actively corrupted by unauthorized parties this way.

Meaning, they cannot *add* transactions, or *alter* them somehow. Only *suppressing*, or *front-running*[91] new transactions by hindering the flow of information. This is called *censoring* and it is bad enough.

A blockchain is trustable code and data, guaranteed to execute.

So, blockchains

1. *guarantee* the correctness of their data, *and*

2. the correctness even of its *future* state changes

which provides for:

1. the trust needed for '*contracts*' to be based on this code and data and

2. for the contracts' *guaranteed* execution along predetermined rules. Which is their code.

If you look at it closely, the blockchain *substitutes* for trust where it is not established, or cannot be established, and so allows for business being conducted as if there was trust.

> ### Blockchains
> *substitute for trust.*

---

91 Front-running: interpreting what a transaction is good for, and beat it to it by an own transaction created on the fly for that purpose.

This is, misleadingly, called *trust-less*, meant as a positive thing. Nerdy term for sure.

Before, this function had to be filled by an intermediary third party, like a notary or escrow service. Or by law, in a weaker, ex-post approach.

Not needed any more. Like CDs.

Blockchains replace intermediaries with mathematics.

There were lots of digital currencies before Bitcoin. But almost all of them were hosted on somebody's main server that tracked the account balances. Every transition had to go through this central server. The Bitcoin makers demonstrated how to get rid of that bottleneck and single point of failure.

But the application of this discovery goes way beyond currency as soon as transactions are allowed to be more than a funds transfer – as Ethereum does allow – and become fully featured, *stateful* program scripts.

Side effects.

So much for the magic. There are side effects.

What is Holding It Back?

The current blockchain implementations will not be the last word. There is research for every wart that has been found.

That does not guarantee though, that a perfect blockchain will be invented one day. And likely, we will see specialized chains that focus on overcoming specific limitations.

Here is what we are facing today.

A blockchain does not guarantee consistency.

And this is trouble. It will change for Ethereum, somewhat.

It's rare to happen but:

> Blockchains, by design,
> can lose data.

Worse yet, they can have data changed because the order of transactions might get re-arranged, in extreme cases rolling back hours or days. Which does not work for financial applications. At least not for banks. Although in fairness they have glitches, too. And then again it works for business cases at scale, e.g. in IoT.

The cause for the possible data–loss is a trade-off inherent to the consensus algorithm. It is directly linked to the way that Bitcoin did away with the central server, i.e. achieves decentralization. Bitcoin pioneered this daring proposition and actually, for Bitcoin, there are no popular plans to ever change this.

What happens, in both Bitcoin and Ethereum, is that the network can sometimes *fork*, or *split*, and stay like this for a while. This happens whenever two or more about equal groups of computers in the network cannot agree what the current state should be, i.e. which transactions are supposedly accepted and executed, and in which order. 'Equal' is defined here by the groups' *hashing power*, i.e. how fast they can collectively calculate answers in the puzzle competition that underlies the proof–of–work consensus algorithm (pg. 144).

The problem then is that depending on which node you ask, you may receive a different answer, e.g. regarding what account has what balance. It can hardly get worse.

In a way these forks happen all the time and programming using a blockchain has to factor this frequent, temporary oscillation of state in.

In those cases, what ensues, is a puzzle competition of *two networks against each other*. One network will be faster in creating new blocks and gradually, nodes from the slower group(s) will defect to the faster group, potentially making it yet faster in that progress, because they add their hashing power to it. This is by design, it's game theory and it's very clever and powerful.

Eventually every node from the slower group will discard their joint belief in what 'the truth' – the world state – was supposed to be, *abandon their state* and join the faster group.

A network split like this can happen by physically cutting off the lines between nodes so that sub–groups are formed that can see only its members but not the others anymore. An intercontinental connectivity problem can cause this, or targeted attacks.

> *Making nodes unreachable* is a major attack vector on blockchains.

The nasty thing is, during a split, you could send a digital payment and be told by the network that your transaction has been processed and registered with the blockchain – even the recommend twelve blocks deep = everything by the book – but it may still always turn out that you got that answer from a node that was part of the smaller group in a network split. And after its defection to the reality of the larger group, it won't remember anything of what it informed you of and told you it had stored into the blockchain. It's all just gone as if it never was.

If you are on the receiving side, you might lose money with dishonest buyers. They might really have sent it, you saw the confirmation and yet all of a sudden, it was not sent at all. It's back in their account.

You might have delivered the goods you owed by that time. Now you're at the mercy of the buyer. To return them or pay again.

Bitcoin had one such catastrophe over the years. Ethereum had a bad split early in pre-beta but such things were honestly expected by everyone to happen and it was fixed fast.

Ethereum is moving towards introducing stronger finality and consistency. Bitcoin looks like it will remain as it is.

A blockchain is not anonymous.

Ownership identification is by 32 to 33 character characters. This is called *pseudonymous*.

It's weaker than anonymity because if one obtains knowledge of a clear name, the pseudonym can be used as link to trace activities past and present. It also helps deducing transaction patterns, even without knowing (yet) who is behind which pseudonym. The patterns can be so clear that they identify the person behind the pseudonym.

Transactions on a blockchain are facilitated between *addresses*. They are the pseudonyms and consist of a pile of letters and numbers, e.g

17fHXHDB8cQhKvoxV2yfUSVo7LGogY7NGR

A transaction in its simplest form holds a *sender address*, a *receiver address* and the *amount* to be sent.

That is all the data there is and if you manage your keys and addresses well, you can achieve a good amount of anonymity through that. There are wallets now that make it easy to never re-use an address, so that it is much harder to collect meta data by means of those addresses. It basically breaks the links up that a pseudonym creates between transactions, by always using a new pseudonym.

It does not cost anything to create new addresses, and so whenever possible, e.g. when receiving money, the wallet creates a new address for you, managing the complexity.

Ethereum and Bitcoin are not confidential.

A transaction's sender and receiver addresses and amount, plus some metadata, is publicly visible, to everyone who has access to the network – because anyone can join it, i.e. add a computer as a regular node.

> ## Anyone can see
> ## every transaction.

When using Bitcoin or Ethereum, the entire data of the blockchain is on each computer that takes part in the mainnet, with no protection. All transactions, all code and all account balances.

As it is right now, there is no getting around that. It is a technical requirement for the basic principles of the blockchain to work. Although Zcash is showing the way forward: how a blockchain transaction can be fully private, with neither addresses nor amounts readable for others.

There are plans to integrate similar cryptography, also based on *zero knowledge proofs*,[92] into Ethereum, using

---

92 *Zero knowledge proofs* give proof for the knowledge about something without giving away what that actual knowledge is. Think someone asks you to prove to them that you have the key to a door, but you don't want to show the key to them. You could instead just demon-

zkSnarks.[93] Opinions differ as to whether Ethereum could ever be protected to the same degree that Bitcoin can, as Ethereum's internal data structure is more explicit than Bitcoin's – as explained above, Bitcoin's blockchain does not actually contain account *balances*, only relative *changes* to the virtual balances. These are easier to encrypt than Ethereum's account balances.

But we are not there yet. Computers and algorithms are also not fast enough yet to make full *homeomorphic encryption* an option for blockchains. That is a truly magic, future form of encryption that allows for computations to be made on *encrypted* data – without decrypting it. And it still takes a long time to create the zkSnarks of Zcash, around a minute per each transaction. For many use cases that can work today, especially for certain types of payment. For many others it's just too slow.

On the other hand, Bitcoin and Ethereum have just not developed to the point that this is incorporated. It is also not on the forefront of concerns of either community. Scaling is the bigger issue.

A blockchain is audit-friendly: past data is verifiable and cannot be tampered. Well, except ...

The combination of transparency and time-stamped hashes, as described above, makes the blockchain an ideal

strate that you can make the door be open or locked at will. The verifier could tell you what to do a couple of times to make sure you really control the key.

93 zkSnarks are a special form of zero knowledge proofs where no interaction between prover and verifier is required. The verifier could *not* ask you explicitly to open or lock the door. A very complex piece of math replaces that interaction.

tool for auditors. This is an unintended consequence, the inventors of Bitcoin would probably have liked it to turn out differently.

There is a misconception among the interested public, and parts of the FBI, that the blockchain would make all things perfectly traceable and non-anonymous. That is not true at all, or rather, only true when it is used wrongly.

However, if you *want* to be traceable, i.e. auditable, the blockchain certainly is your friend. You have verified proof, vouched for by independent and uninterested third parties, for your actions and communications when you do them on the chain and keep using the same address for all of them.

All miners attest with every block they mine to the authenticity of data buried in the earlier blocks beneath, with cryptographically secure signatures.

A blockchain is hard to scale.

The way Ethereum works right now makes it not usable yet for many applications, especially in IoT. For every new client being set up, joining the Ethereum network requires you to download gigabytes of data you are often not really interested in at all.

This will change any day now for Ethereum, with the advent of *light clients*, which receive and hold only the state that is relevant to them.

Although this creates a new question: who should light clients choose to trust? What has to be prevented is a scenario where everyone opts to become a light client, as this would cripple the Ethereum mainnet.

Account numbers are not verified.

Recall that there is no confirmation step when an account is 'created'. In a sense all possible accounts exist.

People have lost millions meanwhile by sending money to wrong accounts – accounts that the blockchain assumes exist, and so accepts the transaction as valid – but that no one has a private key for. Because really it was a mistake and no one on the planet has a key for it or will find it in the next couple of decades. And, yes, the transactions are irrevocable. Sometimes it's a typo, sometimes bugs in the wallet software (open source, no warranties).

The Ethereum guys felt there don't need to be checksum bytes as part of an account number. So any number is valid really as an Ethereum account. And, well, programs have that habit to have bugs and sometimes hold a 0 somewhere they should really have a number.

Says Martin, *"you're not really a blockchain hacker before you haven't lost people a ton of money."*

Then again – some perspective.

While these challenges are real there seem to be surprisingly many business cases where they don't get in the way. It makes sense to zero in on those low–hanging fruits when possible. As long as the reality is mostly that of a technology looking for its application – like it normally should *not* be. But that's the phase we are in.

It's also not like even banks' systems are expected to work flawlessly these days. And in any domain, there are causes for errors and outages that are beyond the protocol's control: hardware, networks, power outages, bugs and sabotage. Those won't go away anytime soon and the possibility of a network fork has to be put into relation to these other possible causes of system failure.

What is a Cryptocurrency?

Bitcoin & company.

The term is used as label for Bitcoin and payment systems that copy the way Bitcoin works. Ethereum now chief among them.

Bitcoin and Ether are cryptocurrencies. They are hardcoded into Bitcoin and Ethereum respectively.

> ### Cryptocurrency is decentralized digital money.

Bitcoin is really the first *decentralized* cryptocurrency, as 'crypto' just stands for 'using cryptography' and virtually every other digital payment systems uses cryptography, including all of the centralized predecessors of Bitcoin. But not in the special way that Bitcoin introduced.

However, the way the term is used today, it really implies decentralization and a system using crypto but not decentralization would not be called a cryptocurrency right now.

Cryptocurrency is a dirty word.

Certainly in the IT and the consultancy industry, the term 'cryptocurrency' used to define what one is *not* interested in.

Many projects make clear that they are about block-chains and smart contracts but *not* about creating or supporting any form of cryptocurrency.

For one, it sounds like Bitcoin, which is not what big corporations want to be associated with, because of its history (see pg. 253). Given that today's cryptocurrencies aren't really *that* crypto, but rather transparent, this takes the word more literal than its current meaning. But of course, there is the inherent challenge to a state monopoly.

And Companies that have customers in the financial industry also don't want to be seen as entering into competition with them by creating a new payment system with unknowable future impact on their core business.

Cryptocurrency powers smart contracts.

There has to be something that smart contracts can send around as payment or they remain toothless. Stopping at some form of mirror asset is like limiting an economy to barter. Not having any form of asset on–chain reduces a blockchain to a new type of (super slow) database.

It is through the fact that blockchains can be used to send real money – in the form of cryptocurrency – that smart contracts acquire their transformative power.

New cryptocurrencies can be created on Ethereum.

That's actually what Ethereum was to a large extent created for (see pg. 70).

Those new cryptocurrencies are also called 'token'. They are different from the *native tokens*, the description reserved for the 'built-in' cryptocurrency of a chain, like Ether or bitcoin.

Can crypto be the better money?

Most people draw a blank, and will freely admit it, on how (normal) money is created, how it really is debt, how much actually exists, how it is leveraged. And how the money one spends for daily needs, or even on a house, is a completely different thing from what is flushing around the globe in hunt of returns.

We won't go into that.

But online fantasy games have long fared very well by having two types of currencies. E.g. 'gold' and 'silver'. One for the every day needs in the life of a game character. Usable for buying standard quality goods, e.g. a well crafted sword. This currency is rather easy to obtain as part of playing the game. One gets it as reward or bounty.

The other type of money is often exceedingly scarce in the game but on offer to buy *for real-world money*. The little but one gets in the game is but to get a taste of it.

It is for buying status symbols, magic weapons, and all kinds of unfair advantages that only a spoiled brat will confuse with winning the game. In other words, it's a huge market.

Online game operators made a killing from selling this premium type of in–game currency. As a business model it was so effective that it killed off almost all studios that did not adapt to it. And there have been the most passionate debates about why the unfair advantages the premium currency buys over other players do not completely kill the game design. To some extent it does. But the reality is that a meta design emerges that rests on the existence of two different types of players: those who pay for the premium currency and those who make do without.

After the financial markets froze over in 2008, people considered whether separating ordinary people's tender from speculative big money this way could be a good idea for real life.

Can a cryptocurrency be a good 'secondary currency?' The normal, less valuable one, the one you buy grocery with? Maybe a house. That you find and spend in a normal life. But don't speculate with?

The tough questions have easy answers with it: it is created by mining, is not debt but has value purely from demand. The supply is known – 16 million bitcoins and 83 million Ether in late 2016 – there is no central bank to create or inflate them and they *cannot* be leveraged.

It's nothing new to have multiple types of currency in use in parallel that have diverse characteristics. It was rather normal just 300 years ago. And money is around for about 5,000.

What is a Digital Currency?

The term 'digital currency' really means a super set of cryptocurrencies. Basically any currency that is based on computer systems and networks, be it centralized or not, using cryptography or not.

But the way the word is used now is to say 'cryptocurrency' without using that dangerous word.

It is largely synonymous at this point.

What is a Digital Asset?

Digital assets represent real-world value.

Digital assets are anything that is somehow tied to real value although it's really just a number floating around in cyberspace.

A balance of cryptocurrency is a digital asset. Company stock or a title for land, stored on the blockchain, are digital assets.

The term used to mean benign files and multi–media content. But in the context of blockchains it has acquired a meaning that is tied to *scarcity*.

Digital assets cannot be copied.

While image files can be copied and it is impossible to say which of the copies would be 'the original' asset, digital assets on the blockchain *cannot* be copied. And it's essential for both cryptocurrencies and *mirror assets* (see below) that they cannot be multiplied.

While it can be said that an image file is an asset only if one has the right to use it, this right is abstract from the digital realm. For an image, your ownership, or right to use, exists independent of whether you have a copy of a file with the image, or who else has a copy. For digital assets however, as understood in the blockchain context, the ability to use the asset is *digitally* restricted as direct expression of the right to use and possibly also the ownership.

Digital Rights Management (DRM) is an attempt to actually achieve something similar for copyrighted material but the requirements are not the same and the technical approaches to DRM are very different from how a blockchain works. They are traditional, in a way, trying to restrict copying. Blockchains copy everything to everyone and create scarcity not by withholding the actual payload.

This is the bearer aspect again that blockchains are designed to enable. It's what the blockchain is about and goes back to how it was invented to prevent double spending of 'digital cash'.

What is a Mirror Asset?

A mirror asset is a digital asset that represents owner-ship of a real-world asset. E.g. mirror assets can be tied to gold, currency, land or stock.

The mirror asset does not have to represent the *paper certificates* of ownership for a scarce good but can double for them:

A mirror asset representing ownership of gold is not per se a new device. Gold has since long been traded by certificates, instead of actually ferrying the gold around. And those certificates can be entirely digital for a while now. So a mirror asset representing gold is different from a digital gold certificate only in that it resides on a block-chain and by virtue of that cannot simply be replicated to do mischief, e.g. sold multiple times to multiple buyers.

The same with company stock. On the blockchain, stock can be implemented as safe, auditable, bearer shares. They need not represent a piece of paper that would qualify as the actual stock. Because a paper stock certi-ficate, already is a mirror-like representation of a fraction of a corporation. It's not the corporation itself. The same is true for gold certificates.

The mirror asset is just making the trade independent of paper. And in the digital domain, independent from a central server that before was needed to make fraud impossible, e.g. by making copies of it and selling it twice.

What is Consensus?

With blockchains, the term 'consensus' has acquired a special meaning.

There are many creative misconceptions about it and this isn't helped by the fact that the *social consensus* between operators and users of a blockchain also plays an important role for the network.

But as a technical term:

> Consensus means that nodes agree on the same world state.

This is difficult to achieve in any computer network.

The Generals' Problem cannot be solved.

In essence the *Byzantine Generals' Problem* says that no two computers can ever be sure that they have the same data.

The metaphor is that two allied generals have to attack at the same time or they will fail. But if their messages to each other can get lost on the way – e.g. for the messenger being captured – there is no way they can be *sure* they have an agreement.

Because, if general Alice sends *"tomorrow, 8am"* to the general Bob, she can't know if Bob got the message. If Bob sends a messenger back acknowledging that he got the message, he can't know if Alice got the acknowledgement.

Therefore it doesn't work to agree beforehand that *"I'll only go as announced if I hear back from you."*

If Alice sent an acknowledgement of the acknowledgement back, she wouldn't be able to know if that arrived either, and so on. There is no way to be sure that a message arrived when the network is unreliable. Because certainty would always depend on another message to arrive back, ad infinitum. And peer–to–peer Internet connections always are unreliable.

Ways have been found to achieve satisfactory certainty using voting rounds, digital signatures and timeouts. Those approaches are designed for more than two parties and utilize majority opinion. They are called *Byzantine fault tolerant consensus protocols*. But they are made for normal database clusters with maybe a dozen nodes. They *might* work for up to around maybe a hundred nodes. After that they become painfully slow because the required communication between all participating nodes gets incredibly complex.

Bitcoin presented a new approach to that problem. Bitcoin and Ethereum in essence forgoe certainty and instead make it the responsibility of each participant to make a best guess on what the majority's best guess will be what the facts are.

What is
Proof-of-Work?

Proof–of–work is the consensus protocol introduced by Bitcoin that makes it possible for thousands of nodes to agree on the world state. Ethereum uses an improved version of it, called *GHOST*, which works on the same premise.

Miners, Validators and Proposers.

Nodes that take part in the consensus building are called *miners* (pg. 157). In *private networks* (pg. 194) – where no mining rewards are given – they can be called *validators*.

A miner or validator that manages to have all things lined up to be able to propose a new block and broadcasts it to the network, is then called *proposer*. Often times, multiple proposals are broadcast at about the same time.

The 'proof of work' is what the other nodes expect to be presented by a proposer together with the block. It's one, special number and proves that the proposer found a solution to a special puzzle.

The whole effort is about how new transactions are added to the chain. Since transactions can come into the network through any node, the challenge is to agree which transactions are processed, and: *in what order.*

In practice, nodes just take the initiative, collect some transactions they heard about into one block and propose it to the other nodes.

The heaviest chain.

This is how proof–of–work keeps thousands of nodes in sync:

> # The responsibility to stay with the majority opinion is *shifted to the node*.

And this is genius.

It's one of the incredibly elegant solutions the Bitcoin makers came up with and that many people now work to get rid off.

Instead of having a negotiation process, this method is letting the proof–of–work algorithm serve as deterrent, punishing unwise decisions: if a node clings to a notion of what the world state should be that later turns out to not be aligned with the rest of the nodes, then all its mining efforts from that moment on will be in vain and it will not be able to secure mining rewards going forward. Therefore, all nodes make a best effort to identify what all other nodes will most likely estimate to be the world state that all other nodes estimate to be the world state (sic).

But there is never a reconciliation step. Never a reset to a status where all nodes explicitly agree on the world state.

Proof-of-work
is non-interactive.

This makes it fast, and allows for the network to scale.

All there ever is, is something called the 'heaviest chain' – the 'longest chain' for Bitcoin.

Nodes on a blockchain get to hear different, conflicting proposals about what the next block should be all the time.

From all proposed blocks and the chains that could be built from them, the heaviest chain is the one that *provably* the most puzzle solving work has been invested into. The proofs are the puzzle solutions that come with the blocks.

The convention is that this heaviest chain is always the chain that reflects 'the truth' of the world state. All 'lighter' chains – concretely, those with fewer blocks, maybe just one less, and a different last block with different transactions or maybe only a different transaction order – are to be rejected.

But this is not just a Schelling point: it is in your best self interest as a miner that if you want to propose a new block you base it on the heaviest chain you know about. Because if you don't, somebody else proposing a new block, which does sit on top of that heaviest chain, will win out and be accepted by the other nodes instead of yours. For the resulting chain's weight of her proposal will be higher than yours.

And that's how it continues, forever.

Proof-of-work incentivizes consensus instead of enforcing it.

That's economic game theory, applied on the very deepest layer of blockchain mechanics, allowing for unprecedented scale. The blockchain community is quite proud of that.

It's also Adam Smith-style selfishness for the greater good replacing the democratic notion of the *part time parliament* of *Paxos*.[94] For efficiency and scale.

There is no rule enforced, which transactions are included in a proposed block.

So, to avoid a situation where everyone only proposes and no one listens, a proposal is only accepted by other nodes when it comes with the solution to a hard-to-solve puzzle.

If anyone would manage to propose all blocks in the network all the time, it would be highly insecure as the proposer has freedom to include any transaction he likes and exclude any he doesn't like. This could lead to *front-running*: exploiting the knowledge about desired transactions by inserting own transactions instead.

There can be no control over who includes which transactions in the first place, because this would require knowledge – and synchronization – about who *knows* about

---

94 Paxos: *"Many computer scientists claim to have read it."* http://research.microsoft.com/en-us/um/people/lamport/pubs/pubs.html#time-clocks

which transactions. This knowledge does not exist in the network.

Proof-of-work is a puzzle competition.

The actual *work* is a continuous puzzle competition against all other nodes in the network. Basically, there is a race on, who is first to find a random number, called *nonce* that gives one the right to propose the next block in the blockchain.

The time any one round lasts is the *blocktime* and is not precisely predictable. Sometimes the number is found faster, sometimes it takes a little longer. It's not really one specific number either, it just has to fulfill a condition in respect to the transactions in your block.

The act of putting a new block together is:

1. take a bunch of transactions you've heard about through the network that are waiting to be put into a block and validate them. Keep the valids

2. put a random number to them, the *nonce*

3. hash all of that

4. then check the *leading zeros* of that hash (!)

5. if your hash, coincidently really, has the required number of leading zeros, you are done and can propose the block, attaching the nonce as your proof of work.

6. otherwise, retry from 2.

Concretely, the nonce you try first could be 0, changing it for the next attempt can simply mean to increment it. There is no specific rule. The number of zeros required could e.g. be 12, and this is called the current *difficulty*. It is normal to need trillions of iterations to find a nonce with the right number of leading zeros. Leading zeros are not normally of interest with hashes. This is quite a special way to use them.

There is no way to predict how long the race will last or who will be the winner. The latter is an important feature.

The trap-door again.

At the heart of this scheme is the fact that a nonce is hard to find but easy to verify. While it routinely takes trillions of trial-and-error calculations to find it, it requires but one calculation to verify it: to test that a nonce is in fact resulting into a hash with the required number of leading zeros when added to the block data that it was found for.

But even trillions of calculations would amount to a mere blip for modern CPUs if the hash algorithm was as simple as calculating a cross sum. It factors that a hash algorithm itself costs a little bit of time to calculate.

The Hash Rate.

The total gear employed across the network to solve these puzzles determines the total *hash rate*[95] of the network. It changes over time as miners join or leave the network. The higher it is, the better is the network protected against attacks.

---

95   Ethereum hash rate – https://etherscan.io/charts/hashrate

At the end of 2016 it was at 8 Tera Hashes per second for Ethereum, meaning 8 trillion hashes are tried each second across the network to find a nonce.

Which means that about every 100 trillionth hash is found to be a usable nonce.

For Bitcoin[96] the numbers are still wilder, 2 Exa Hashes per second, so about every sextillionth hash is a hit.

The hash rates are so high because making money this way – mining – became a business lucrative enough to see the emergence of professional miners who invest millions into hardware build small server farms specifically to mine.

Proof-of-work uses insane amounts of electricity.

The puzzle to be solved, and the found nonce, are completely useless per se and it's a bit painful how much electricity is gorged up by miners doing so. For Bitcoin it is around an eye-popping $300 million a year, which is about the electricity bill of all of Ireland. There are entire hydro-electric power plants being dedicated almost fully to Bitcoin mining, in China, the availability of which has lead to a concentration of Bitcoin hashing power in China.

Admirable efforts are under way to use this calculation power for something useful besides protecting the network, e.g. finding signs of cancer in scans. But this noble thinking can probably not work, because as soon as the electricity is not wasted anymore, the mining becomes economically 'free', which would reduce the protection it lends to the blockchain. In that sense, many argue, it has to stay as wasteful as it is and should not be considered a waste in the first place.

96   Bitcoin hash rate – https://blockchain.info/charts/hash-rate

The Space of Useless Hashes.

The creation of all the useless hashes can be seen as what projects value into Cypherspace, the meaningless noise making the few hits valuable. Like all the empty space around the tiny specks of matter in the real world. With the hash function that is being executed over and over, projecting infinity to the finite, as part of the process of creating the paradox of digital scarcity.

There is a similar weirdness in online games, where a common pattern in game design, called *grind*, is to require players to do 'work' in the game that is repetitive, boring and costs real time, to acquire valuables in the game world.

In this way, real–world time is translated into in–game value. It is perplexing in that it seems to go against all reasons why one would play a game. But it likewise imbues value by wastefulness.

As an alternative to grind, one can often buy one's way out of it with real–world money.

And *that* looks very similar to how proof–of–stake might replace proof–of–work. Instead of spending millions for buying blockchain mining hardware and electricity, miners might in the future just bond real money to the blockchain to acquire a slice of proposer rights.

What is
Proof-of-Stake?

There is an effort under way, funded by the Ethereum Foundation, to find a better way. It is called proof–of–stake and is based on the principle of bonds.

> Proof–of–stake may replace the wasteful, centralizing proof–of–work.

Instead of rewarding the winner of a senseless race for a random number, with proof–of–stake, a miner who violates certain rules would lose money. That's his stake. There are still rewards for creating blocks but they are dished out round-robin to all who participate, because the responsibility to create the next block goes round-robin.

The term *proof–of–stake* is a bit of a pun on *proof–of–work*, but the 'work' here and the 'stake' there are not used to prove the same thing, at all:

The *work* of proof–of–work is to make it expensive to create the next block, so that the fact that you have a chain of blocks, with work gone into making each block, makes it hard to forge such a chain. The harder the longer the chain is.

The *stake* of proof–of–stake on the other hand is a bond that the chain holds for every miner, which makes it possible to punish behavior that *sustains a split* – a state of non–consensus – instead of helping to heal it. This becomes relevant when two or more groups of nodes can, for a time, not agree which block should be the next block. Nodes are under the obligation then to decide for one side, no matter which, at the threat of losing their bond if they *ride the bandwagon on both*. Which would in the instance mean, to propose new blocks for both sides of the split. If they are found out doing this, they lose their bond.

Such split can happen by a partial breakdown of the communication in the network, or because a node that was supposed to create the next block went down in that very moment. Really it happens all the time in Ethereum, as opposed to Bitcoin, because of Ethereum's fast block times and the important point is just to force all participants in the network to immediately make a decision which side of the fork they want to support and not go forward working with both sides.

With proof–of–work, a miner working both sides of a fork would simply reduce her chances to ever get a block reward, as she would split up her puzzling power between two targets, effectively halving it. So the penalty for sup-porting both sides becomes the loss in rewards. That's sufficiently elegant.

With proof–of–stake, a miner who is detected to work for both sides, would lose her bond. Where bonds might themselves be held back prior mining rewards. Using bonds makes the on-boarding and off-boarding process for miners a lengthier process, to make sure they cannot game the system and to not create an incentive to split the net-work in skillful ways to avoid the loss of their bond. It has to be made sure that they really have 'something at stake'.

What is a Hard-Fork?

A hard–fork is a code update to the clients running on the blockchain nodes that makes transactions valid that previously weren't. And/or vice versa: transactions invalid that previously were deemed valid.

> A hard–fork
> can re–write history.

This can be used to reverse very specific transactions, e.g. undo thefts, or fix vulnerabilities of the transaction processing core that can be exploited by attacks on the network.

For a hard–fork, all node owners have to decide wether they want to take part in the upcoming changes or leave things as they are. To take part, the nodes have to be stopped and a code upgrade has to be performed by the owner of the node.

A hard–fork always forks the blockchain up between the group of nodes who run the upgraded code and those who stayed behind. Technically it always results into two blockchains although the hope is usually that the old variant will die fast, which basically happens as soon as no node runs the old code anymore. They can always be revived, however. Hard–forks create zombies.

Hard–forks were used a couple of times in Ethereum's history, first to revert The DAO heist (pg. 286), later to fix vulnerabilities that were exploited for attacks.

One could argue that they defeat the purpose of Ethereum in that it was designed to allow for adding features – i.e. types of transactions – without having to stop, upgrade and restart the nodes.

However, code upgrades – without hard–forks – are a frequent and expectable event for Ethereum nodes. The clients are constantly being improved: performance–optimized, made more robust or receiving new peripheral features that are not part of the core blockchain functionality.

On the other hand, Bitcoin never had a real hard–fork. And the original vision for Ethereum had been to take nodes down as rarely as possible.

What is Mining?

Mining is finding the next block.

Mining is taking part in the proof–of–work puzzle competition.

Finding a suitable nonce gives the right to propose the next block of transactions to the network, as well as to collect the transaction fees from the transactions and write a block reward to oneself – 5 Ether or 12 bitcoin – into that block.

The reward is why it is called 'mining', it's where the money from nothing is created.

Mining made people rich.

Because you can earn handsome rewards for it. The days that you could use your personal hardware to mine are over for Ethereum, too.

For Ethereum mining, you need GPUs. The developers tried to avoid a situation like with Bitcoin, where special hardware – *ASICs*[97] – can be made that leaves anyone in the dust who tries to mine without it. But Ethereum

---

97 Application-specific integrated circuit: chips that are specialized at doing exactly one thing, faster than software can do it on normal hardware. In this case: mining Bitcoins.

mining gear is highly specialized hardware at this point, too.

Mining is sustaining and protecting the network.

As a miner you help the blockchain to process its transactions. You *package transactions into blocks and propose them to the network* as next block. And you also verify that blocks that other miners proposed make sense.

To mine Ethereum, you simply start a node in mining mode. This entails that all calculations of all transactions that happen on the blockchain, no matter who initiated them, will be performed on your computer. And that any storage space that is used by anyone to store values in a blockchain script, will also be stored on your computer.

That is true for every full Ethereum node though, mining or not. Though in the near future only *full clients* and *miners* will do this and *light clients* will not.

But your mining node would also enter into the proof–of–work competition, trying to, faster than anyone else, find a possible next block to be added on top of the blockchain.

Mining protects the network against DDOS attacks and unauthorized state changes.

So the winner of the proof–of–work puzzle competition is simply who finds a fitting nonce first and can show it to the other nodes.

Effectively this is a *leader selection* in the consensus process: the luckiest puzzler gets to be the leader, earning the right to propose what the next state progress of the block-chain should be.

The important part here is that this way of leader election is *completely unpredictable* and thus, no-one can target the coming block proposer, and by this stall the entire network. Because the next proposer is unknown and unknowable in advance.

Each miner also adds to the total hash rate of the network and the higher this is, the harder does it become to take the network over by pure calculation power.

Mining costs stabilize cryptocurrencies.

The cost of mining is probably influencing the price of bitcoin and Ether, in a good way. Miners seem to be hording their rewards and sell them as soon as they can break even with electricity cost. This stabilizes the bitcoin price, which makes Bitcoin less interesting for speculators and more useful as currency.

These dynamics will change as the Bitcoin system is programmed to phase out block rewards over the years until miners sole reward will come from transaction fees. This establishes an upper limit for the number of bitcoins that will come into existence.

Ethereum keeps block rewards steady and will not phase them out, leading to a constant increase in money supply for Ether.

What is Decentralized Code?

Decentralized code is a program running on a blockchain.

This means, it is *hosted identically* on thousands of computers and *executed in parallel* on all of them. And therefore, not depending on any one single computer to run it.

If a network node goes down or refuses to execute the code, it is still executed on all the other nodes.

This is what gives it mainframe-like robustness and reliability. But what's more, it also does not have an off switch.

Decentralized code cannot be altered or shut down.

Note that the term 'decentralized code' is descriptive and not part of the established canon of terms. As opposed to, say, 'smart contracts', 'Dapps' or 'blockchain'. The concept is central but it does not really have a widely used name at this point.

Decentralized code is deployed to the blockchain by a transaction.

Any code that ends up on the blockchain gets there as part of a transaction.

In Bitcoin, on the technical level, every transaction carries code that is mixed with previous transactions' code to create the script for the actual action: the test of signatures and the transfer of the money. The transaction itself is really phrased in code.

In Ethereum, code is something in its own right and is deployed in the form of a parameter that is assigned to a transaction that is sent to the blockchain specifically to deploy that piece of code. The code is then usable for anyone who learns about it.

Decentralized code is verifiable as to its correctness by all.

Decentralized code inherits this from the basic features of the blockchain. Everything about transactions on the blockchain is out in the open, everyone with access to the blockchain itself can see all transactions that ever happened. This will change in the future but at least with the technology we have now, this introduces a striking transparency.

To recap, the cause for this is that, for every node in the network to be able to execute all transactions, all information – data and code – has to be shared. And, this was not a design choice, but is a necessity for the basic blockchain mechanism to work (see pg. 119).

Decentralized code is revision safe.

What is true for the data on the blockchain is true for the code on it as well: once something is recorded on the blockchain, no one can alter or remove it without obviously breaking everything.

It's a side effect but has taken on a life of its own as a great feature of blockchains that provides *revision safety*.

Results of decentralized code are double checked constantly and thousands of times.

The results of every single execution of decentralized code end up on the blockchain, too. Including its logs and all cross–contract calls it may have triggered. So everyone can check at any time whether the produced results are correct.

And in fact, as we discussed, that *is* exactly what the nodes in the Ethereum network do all the time: checking, for themselves, what the results of *everyone elses* input to the network should be. It's a core principle. It gives the results of decentralized code a unique reliability on the long tail that before, only mainframes could offer as default.

Decentralized code cannot call URLs.

Meaning, it cannot call out to read a web page, or pull data from a server on the Internet, or really make any request that reaches beyond the horizon of their blockchain network.

This is true, by extension, for smart contracts.

Recall that decentralized code is executed identically on thousands of nodes and it is crucial that every node comes to the same result (pg. 90, 100).

If calling out from the network would be allowed and only one node could not reach said URL, or the URL gave different results back to different nodes, this would kick all nodes off the network that – for the different or non–answer they got – don't arrive at the majority opinion result.

It could destroy the complete network in seconds if the URL call gave *every* node a different result.

Not to speak of the latency the call would add. Decentralized code is slow enough, you don't really want to add wait–time on top for interacting with external sources.

But there is a way.

External calls are done by control flow inversion.

This means that when you really need to pull a value, if you can't pull in the first place, you have to create a structure so that the value ends up being pushed to you.

The way it works is by:

1. writing the URL – or often just a part of it – into the blockchain, as value,

2. let it be read by an off-chain service that pulls for such values,

3. that calls the URL, and

4. writes the result back on to the blockchain for the decentralized code to read.

What is a Dapp?

A Dapp is a *decentralized application* that uses decentralized code.

Dapps are very much what Ethereum was made for. Their main feature is decentralized code and they inherit its exciting attributes.

A Dapp has a decentralized backend and a centralized front end.

The backend of a Dapp will at least partially be code and storage on a blockchain. That's what gives it the name and makes essential parts of it ultra robust and trustworthy. Both in technical terms and in business terms: the parts on the blockchain cannot be altered retroactively and every change going forward is in the open.

But the front-end – the user interface, graphics, web pages or mobile apps – will usually be served in a traditional way, coming from centralized servers or cloud services.

Because of the performance and capacity limits of today's blockchains, large parts of the *backend* of a Dapp – databases and business logic – will also be hosted on centralized servers or cloud services.

Ethereum is a platform for building Dapps.

BitTorrent and Bitcoin could be called Dapps. They are decentralized applications with a clear, singular purpose.

Ethereum is a general purpose–Dapp platform, made to allow for things to be built on it, which have the same basic, decentralized goodness that makes Bitcoin and Bit-Torrent powerful.

What is a Smart Contract?

I heard two of the most core people of Ethereum quip:

"I don't know what a smart contract is."

The term is used in a very blurry way sometimes. But the following should give you a clear sense of what makes a smart contract, with a view not limited to the context of Ethereum.

The idea of a more precise law.

The term 'smart contract' was coined by Nick Szabo before Bitcoin, purportedly in 1994. That's why some people believe that he might be *Satoshi Nakamoto*, the mystical, unknown inventor of Bitcoin.[98]

Szabo's idea was to codify a legal agreement in a program and have a computer execute its terms instead of humans having to interpret and act on it. Szabo hoped, most of all, for a more precise form of jurisdiction.

---

98 It was probably Hal Finney though, whose health curve correlated with Nakamoto's verbosity. And who kept his Bitcoins to have them when he gets unfrozen.

Now with blockchains we can have exactly that! And arguably a whole lot more, because the blockchain makes the contract program *unstoppable* and gives it the power to directly *move money* with no one able to interfere.

And that makes them something new.

Smart contracts are agreements with super powers.

The magic formula here is a combination of three powerful effects.

A smart contracts is an agreement that is binding, not only in theory but in practice as it can move information *and* money around based on the concrete terms of the agreement.

It is unstoppable, an 'automatism' that is guaranteed to resolve itself, Not resting on a legal system and its enforcement but on the blockchain instead.

And it is way more precise and arguably easier to read than legal texts and the millions of pages of rules that define their actual meaning.

A smart contract is decentralized code that moves money based on a condition.

Any decentralized code can move money, i.e. cryptocurrency, or effect some other type of exchange, e.g. of digital assets. Smart contracts are decentralized code that does so *after a condition* is fulfilled.

It can be a set of very complex conditions, there can be interdependencies between smart contracts. They can be extremely short or long running. The condition can be internal to the blockchain or fed in from the outside.

It doesn't matter, at some point a set of conditions will be fulfilled and the contract will pay out. Or refund.

Ethereum and Bitcoin have cryptocurrency built–in and smart contracts will usually use them to make a payment that is final quickly.

A smart contract could also trigger a payment through traditional means, say initiating a credit card payment or use Paypal, instead of using Ether or bitcoin for payment. But that's not quite the same, the true power of a smart contract unfolds when it can transfer digital assets directly. Because that is when it's effect really becomes (almost) unstoppable.

A smart contract is guaranteed to execute.

Specifically, a smart contract is independent of the parties taking part in a transaction, and perfectly isolated from any change of heart. Simply because it is decentralized code.

Once things are set in motion, the blockchain underneath serves as an independent third party and makes sure that what was agreed upon in the code will be executed.

No recharges, no second thoughts, no legal tricks, arm twisting or delayed payments. This can level the playing field for small businesses and make their lives tremendously much better.

It can save big business billions and make markets lucrative that have no reliable paths of litigation.

Smart contracts might become a form of law.

But they certainly are not yet. Right now, they are some scary other thing and the word 'contract' merely stands for the resolve that stands at its beginning, not for a legal agreement in meat–space.

A smart contract is not necessarily between two parties, and in reality almost never, so far, the mirror image or replacement of a legal contract.

Now, if two parties were to tell a judge today that what they meant to agree upon is reflected in a piece of code then the judge might agree that this piece of code constitute a contract.

But as it is at present, there can instead be a problematic gap opening up any time, between what a smart contract can – irreversibly – effect and what is legal. Or what the actual intention was.

The DAO debacle (pg. 286), instead of simplifying things and dying with flying flags, brought us discussions about a fourth dimension besides the *letter of the law*, the *spirit of the law* and, *code is law*: all of a sudden the *spirit of the code* was discussed after the code was discovered to have had a flaw! Aw.

A smart contract can deliver digital goods.

Decentralized code can facilitate distribution of music videos or news over the Internet. The trigger for delivery would be a signed transaction pushed to the blockchain and in the simple, straight forward case you would not call that a smart contract yet.

But as soon as the delivery would be in response to a more complex interaction, involving some proof of eligibility, or a tit-for-tat deal, you would call the code a smart contract.

There could be digital money coming in as payment, bitcoin, or Ether. Or a proof for payment made outside the blockchain, by traditional means. Or it could be in reaction to any other state change within the blockchain's horizon, e.g. a blockchain game.

A smart contract can trigger delivery of real-world goods and services.

While the more powerful scenario for a smart contract is to govern strictly virtual goods, they can certainly be about business in the real world.

They can trigger the delivery of real things ordered, earned or paid for on the blockchain. They can be used to reliably ping web sites, send emails or effect on-demand prints of books, anything that a program can initiate today, or that you could do through a web site.

A smart contract can be triggered by an *external* condition.

This is the usual situation for smart contracts, they will be tied to *external* events and they are set in motion by receiving a signed transaction expressing what the outcome of a specific event was. In the case of Ethereum this transaction is a call of a method of the smart contract itself, coming from an externally operated account (EOA, see pg. 86).

This transaction will usually be initiated by a tightly controlled, local system that is not part of the blockchain. This system will create automatic signatures for the data it then feeds into the blockchain by means of the EOA.

If that sounds complicated – it isn't, it's just how the real world is having an effect on the blockchain in a secure way.

A smart contract can function as independent, verifiable middle-man.

Because of the nature of decentralized code, smart contracts can be trusted to do what they are proposed to do, without having to trust the people behind them. Just looking at the code is enough.

And smart contracts can be trusted to pull it through even if it hurts, as they can't really be stopped.

Therefore, smart contracts are magnitudes more reliable, easier to vet and cheaper than existing middlemen structures.

No cheating, no bribes, no blackmailing, no rent seeking. Awesome. At least when handling values that are interesting for normal people and businesses.

Middlemen will not go away, they will become operators of this technology, earn a lot less and find relief from certain temptations. And while one could claim that there are unintended benefits in crypto for the underworld mafia, it is for sure bad for the established, official one.

A smart contract can dis–intermediate intermediaries in any market.

Blockchain technology makes business intermediaries redundant the same way that the Internet itself made physical carriers of entertainment redundant – laser discs in the instance.

The music industry had carved out a nice niche around the bottle neck they controlled, the distribution of physical media, and had a real hard time realizing that this was going away.

After failing to make everyone believe that they had been around forever as enabler of mankind – and not basically only for 50+ years – they simply went back to focus on a less scalable part of the business, throwing concerts.

> ## Smart contracts
> *dis-intermediate the intermediaries.*

Across all industries, the blockchain will make any form of being the 'trusted intermediary' in business lose value and will force players in escrow, law, insurance and banking to regroup around services that are more directly value creating and less rent seeking.

Similar to the music business, what will be taken out of the financial classes hands might simply be the 50 years old advantage, and expectable glut, that came with global telecommunication. The interesting arc is that cryptography itself was allowed to be used in business only 50 years ago, to secure the new way of doing business, based on telecommunication. Now crypto might be used to undo some of the advantages corporations gained with the advent of telecommunication.

Banking used to be boring. For the benefit of many, it might just become boring again.

A smart contract can create a market.

The most amazing thing about smart contracts is that they can enable markets where in the past the overhead to create one had been too big.

They can help open up niches for people to trade where there was no exchange, no sharing of information and no common ground. Simply by shielding people from things going awry and eliminating opportunities to cheat.

> Smart contracts allow for new markets by forcing honesty.

They don't enforce honesty after the fact, they force everyone to be honest from the get go.

No third party is needed for escrow. Money is guaranteed to flow on contract resolution, without need to ever sue for it. You can establish a sustainable form of justice, without judges, lawyers and court fees.

Smart contracts may also have a strong, sorry impact on society by augmenting the possibilities for commoditization of things that should not be regarded as tradable goods in the first place.

Mankind will not be able to keep itself from experimenting. And if we are just too stupid, maybe we deserve the consequences. After that, the true value–backlash, blockchain–supported!

Smart contracts live on the blockchain.

They inherit the limitation of decentralized code:

> ## Smart contracts cannot reach information outside the blockchain.

Like decentralized code they can really only get pushes, they cannot pull. But because pushes and pulls can be inversed this is not a crippling limitation.

A smart contract has less bells and whistles than a Dapp.

Smart contracts and Dapps live in slightly different dimensions. A Dapp is more across the board and closer to a product. A smart contract is closer to pure logic.

A Dapp has parts that live on the blockchain and other parts: it will often include dynamic web pages or a mobile app and a database backend. A Dapp is the 'full package' that makes a useful product, including all interfaces for the end user, and most of that will be centrally hosted.

With smart contracts, we are looking at a smaller radius, the term means only those parts that live on the blockchain. Backends of Dapps can consist of, use, or create smart contracts. Smart contracts can be visualized or managed by Dapps. But a smart contract per se does not have a front end.

The Fallacy of Naive Modeling.

> One smart contract will almost never replace exactly one legal contract.

Many simple and clean architectures are proposed these days that basically project an agreement from the real world onto a smart contract, very much 1:1. It can make a lot of sense to design a system thinking along these lines. But in the end, real applications are almost never going to look like this.

Designing applications in this naive style is not unique to blockchains. Many books about *object orient programming* have examples featuring vehicles, cars and car parts to illustrate the principle of inheritance versus aggregation. However, no real program ever had a car object inherited from a vehicle base class that aggregated wheel objects. Maybe with the exception of a video game.

But by and large the actual implementation of a system looks way less literal. It uses software patterns, optimizations and instrumentation[99] that break the 1:1 abstraction up and obscure the abstracted reality in the code.

---

[99] Code that makes it possible to better inspect what the program is doing while it is running to increase security, tune performance and find bugs.

For smart contracts, the immediate issues are testing, monitoring, cost of execution, upgradability and performance.

For example, imagine you deployed a thousand smart contracts to the blockchain that are all of the same type and so all have the same code and represent a thousand real-world agreements. Then if you found an honest mistake in one that everyone agrees should be fixed, you would have to fix the code a thousand times. There *are* scenarios where you might want to have it that way. But most of the times, this would just be error prone and costly. So an implementation looks more sensible that uses just one smart contract and thus, one code deployment to the blockchain, which is programmed in a way so it can run the thousand different real-world agreements by accepting different data parameters. When the code has to be fixed – as more complex programs practically always have to be at one point – there is only one instance of it that has to be swapped out.

So the assumption that one contract will be deployed, object-like, as one code instantiation that has one static state, will not hold. If it is of any comfort, those entities that feed the data to the code will likely also be smart contracts. Just simpler ones with only feeder logic and not the actual business logic as their code.

In Ethereum, 'smart contract' often just means 'a Solidity script'.

As noted before, the term 'smart contract' has taken on a bit of a life of its own in Ethereum, as 'contract' became to mean any script really in Ethereum, since the name for a 'class' of even the simplest Solidity program is literally called 'contract.' So the term *smart contract* is often used synonymously with 'contract class', or 'contract instance'.

But there is a world outside Ethereum and a *smart contract* should be understood as described above.

Smart contracts are computer code.

There is also a very interesting but totally different use of the term 'smart contracts' pushed by Barclay's[100] that is about management of the complete lifecycle of legal contracts, especially to make it easier to create and interpret them. Their execution is *not* necessarily done by a computer and the focus is the creation of *legal prose*.[101]

While the full name of the concept is 'Smart Contract Templates', predictably this definition can be used to propose that ledgers, which store *the text* of legal contracts that were created this way, feature smart contracts.

But these Templates are really something else completely and the purpose of their results – human readable contract text – is to be 'legally enforceable', in court. While the whole point of smart contracts on the blockchain is that they enforce themselves.

The hugely relevant overlap with blockchain is that concepts like the Templates are the required work to standardize legal text creation, and match it with co-created program code, so smart contracts can be guaranteed to be legal, readable by lawyers, too, rather than only coders, and tap into the legal system as backstop. The duality of

---

100 'Smart Contract Templates' –
https://arxiv.org/pdf/1608.00771v2.pdf

101 *"Although some groups are actively pursuing tamper-proof smart contract code, our preference is for smart legal contracts that are enforceable by traditional legal methods"* – ibid.

legal text and program code, generating both out of a single source, could become a main avenue towards realizing the full potential of blockchains.

Which does not take away from the benefits of scale, fairness, low cost and overhead that real smart contracts have over legal contracts.

Smart contracts are math.

They deal in scarcity – set amounts of cryptocurrency or digital assets – and yet are independent of any concrete representation. They are *not* like the electrons currently signifying your money on your bank account. Granted there will be back ups and double checks in place. But *if* those electrons disappeared, your money would, too.

The reason that smart contracts are different is because they do not represent a value – like a bank account – but math. They are independent of any concrete value the same way that $y = 2x$ is a valid statement independently of what the real number x is.

> ### Smart contracts are part of one big formula: the complete chain.

The input to that formula are the transactions, all of them signed and smart contracts themselves come into the chain by transactions. Their code is itself input to the chain.

When they run, they are but part of the bigger computation of the current world state, calculated from the genesis block. One long computation that never quite stops but always has a current endpoint in the latest block.

The input data, including all code, is what the chain consists of. It is complete and it is unambiguous what the result at each block is.

Smart contracts have no location.

That smart contracts are executed symmetrically, the exact same way on thousands of nodes, really makes them have no physical location.

> ## Smart contracts live
> ## in Cypherspace.

The electrons signifying your money in the bank are actually locatable. Technically.

A smart contract running on thousands of computers at about the same time gets much harder to physically pin down. Especially when it doesn't matter if you take any or even a lot of nodes out. How it will still continue, perfectly unphased, on the rest of the nodes, shows how it is not dependent on any specific bit of matter. Pun intended.

What is a DAO?

Here comes the science fiction bit.

(For the *The* DAO, see pg. 286.)

A DAO is a decentralized, autonomous organization.

You could *manage* a company using the blockchain. The Ethereum Foundation itself, and Joe Lubin's Consensys are about to try some of that. *Slock.it*[102] were pushing for this.

But the idea of a DAO is that you can create a *completely independent entity that is exclusively governed by the rules that you program into it and 'lives' on the chain*.

This is more than using the blockchain to manage a company: instead, the code *is* the entire company. And it cannot be stopped.

It does not matter whether it is incorporated or not. It is an organization.

---

102 Slock.it is a company that utilizes Ethereum to create access controls, smart locks, for the sharing economy – https://slock.it

A DAO consists of complex smart contracts.

In terms of Ethereum, a DAO will usually be a bunch of smart contracts, not only one, which interact to provide the functionality of the DAO.

So here is what we have:

> Decentralized code → smart contract → DAO.

Decentralized code: trustworthy because hard to stop.

Smart contract: decentralized code moving money.

DAO: smart contracts forming a business entity.

A DAO sustains itself.

A DAO could deal in anything and it could also be a regular, legal business entity one day. It could live longer than its creator.

It could run and own a hotel: hire and fire people scanning it's own Yelp ratings, procure whatever is needed for daily operations using the Ethereum mainnet and leverage smart building technology to offer the best possible experience for guests.

Or think of a self-driving car that takes care of itself: it will have a budget, maybe in bitcoin, to pay for needed service that its sensors would tell it about. It would take part in an Uber-like network as a self-employed machine. A robot really, though not looking quite like we expected. To make the transition easier, of course a talking puppet could be installed in the driver's seat, mechanic hands glued to the token steering wheel.

Why not! Imagine. Considering how people now get shot from the skies by remote controlled, flying robots on a daily basis, with reputable newspapers giving space to the argument this is a good thing, it should not be too hard to imagine something nice coming from all the progress in automation, for a change.

Like a friendly, knowledgeable, well driving taxi driver who is not bent on ruining your first day after landing in a foreign country by fleecing you as hard as he can.

Or, should it figure out this particular optimization all by itself, at least it gave you reason to marvel at its AI and enjoy the ride.

A DAO owns digital assets.

This can be Ether, bitcoin, domain names, shares of other DAOs, or *synthetic assets* mirroring real–world assets such as precious metals or derivatives.

A DAO *could* also be a Digger-style[103] thing that inter-acts with other digital entities and the real-world strictly on non-monetary basis.

But most of the time a DAO without its own funds would merely be regarded as a smart contract, not a DAO. Any collection of smart contracts can just be a function library, if it does not have a 'life on its own'.

To really be in the game, a DAO will need a budget. This is not surprising as public blockchains are all about economic incentives.

_____

103 Diggers created a world free of money and capitalism in the 60's.

Bitcoin and Ethereum are DAOs.

This is a different way of looking at what a DAO is: one could say that Bitcoin, Ethereum and other block-chains that carry value are actually DAOs themselves.

And many business usecases talk about using a DAO these days when they want to issue a coin. In that sense our HelloCoin example was a DAO smart contract: it can sustain itself and it has funds that it governs. The funds are even in a currency it controls completely. And it does not do much more than controlling it.

So that's a special form of a DAO, one that is structurally very similar to coding an entire business operation into the blockchain but a lot simpler, focussing only on being the nexus for a new currency.

A DAO provides useful service to the real world or other DAOs.

A DAO is expected to be in the business of something and interact with the real world, or at least with the virtual world.

The most powerful constellation here is, like with smart contracts, if the dealings of the DAO stay completely in the digital realm. Like a DAO selling files for download, providing information, entertainment, or sensor data.

This allows for the entire business cycle to be under direct control of the code it consists of. It does not have to delegate and trust on anyone else, e.g. for goods to arrive, on certificates to come in, on credit card payments to be paid out etc.

A DAO buys services from the real world or other DAOs.

The more interesting DAOs will take part in the real–world economy as buyers and sellers. A download service DAO would also go out and look for deals to buy, to offer them to its own customers then. Otherwise, if it were to only sell, that might not yet pass as completely autonomous.

A DAO might own a washer and offer washing services, procuring detergent and mechanical service as needed. It would be making money on the tiny margins to be made from this and always in danger of going out of business if it fails to insure its rolling stock.

A DAO has major legal challenges.

A DAO could have need to spend money for its own lawyers.

At this point in time, the reality of self-executing contracts, or entire autonomous business entities existing exclusively on the blockchain, *"directly conflicts with the architecture and gatekeeping functions of our current legal frameworks,"* says Constance Choi of Seven Advisory,[104] who was the co-founder of one of the first Bitcoin exchanges.

Someone needs to own a DAO, someone needs to be held responsible in case something goes wrong. But a DAO can be created anonymously. It can own money that is not controlled by anybody except its rules that might be unchangeable. And there are business models emerging that bank on exactly that.

---

104 Seven Advisory – http://www.sevenadvisory.com

The discussion in legal circles goes into the direction that this might result into laws having to change, to accommodate the new reality. Primavera and Constance like to call this issue *"the law of the horse versus the law of the platypus,"* in reference to the 90's discussion about whether the advent of Cyberspace required a new type of law.[105]

The question is, whether existing rules should or even *can* be applied to a new phenomenon that is qualitatively so different from all that came before. Or whether new rules have to be created to do justice to a new animal that is so substantially different, even if parts of it look like something we saw before.

When Gavin Wood, of York and EthCore, compares blockchain tech to a force of nature, the argument goes that it will not matter, what is deemed legal or not, blockchains will simply work. Law might have to deal with it, not the other way around.

A DAO might find that crime pays best.

Of course, a DAO could be programmed to optimize itself. And unless protective measures are programmed into its rules, nothing keeps a DAO from finding out that a criminal action pays best. This could be a statistical result from A-B tests. Or an optimization without good sense for some obvious circumstances that no human would fail to recognize as against the law. Not to speak of morals.

And you'll recall, the vision was that DAOs are unstoppable.

---

105 Lawrence Lessig: *The Law of the Horse: What Cyberlaw Might Teach,* 1999 – https://cyber.harvard.edu/works/lessig/finalhls.pdf

A DAO will by default have no ethics.

If you program decisions, you might also have to program ethics into smart contracts. We'll have ethics bugs. And ethic bugs that are features. It won't get boring.

Self-driving cars have this problem now. It's anyone's guess how the programmers of tactical systems value the life of the driver vs. that of pedestrians getting in the way.

Like, maybe if it's only one driver and five people in danger on the sidewalk, why not steer the car off the bridge?

This won't happen but how do we reason about these cases?

What is an Oracle?

This is yet another term that people like to use in different ways. As a technical term, it originally comes from cryptography where it signifies a truly random source, e.g. of a random number. This provides the necessary gate from a crypto equation to the world beyond. As within an algorithm, there simply cannot be randomness.

And this *gate to the beyond*, the real world, is what '*oracle*', at large, has acquired as meaning in the blockchain world.

> Oracles feed smart contracts information from beyond the chain.

The range of what people regard as an oracle is broad. It can be the sensor of an IoT device, but also web services that provide information in a format suitable for smart contracts to consume.

Oracles are interfaces from the real to the digital world.

A smart contract often needs to be able to learn about things happening in the real world. Say it's a Will, then it needs to be triggered after the person setting it up deceased. This information has to reach the blockchain somehow. Or else the contract, however elaborate, won't be of any use.

An oracle is a source of such required real–world information. And as such it will often be the trigger for crucial state changes in the digital reality – especially for smart contracts to resolve themselves and e.g. make a payout.

A detergent sensor of a washing machine that is operated by a DAO might act as fact base for an oracle. This washer might have ordered detergent and will be satisfied that the delivery arrived, and make the required payment, when it learns that this sensor indicates that detergent has been refilled.

Oracles can be services that give out digital proof for any event that happened.

As long as it can be expressed as yes/no, number or text, an oracle can serve up any answer to any question.

There exist services now, like *Oraclize*[106] and *RealityKeys*,[107] which offer concrete implementations of the concept and strive to provide facts for the blockchain in useful ways.

---

106 Oraclize – http://www.oraclize.it/

107 RealityKeys – https://www.realitykeys.com/

Oraclize is part smart contract, part web service and functions like an API to the real world that can be polled from an Ethereum smart contract and that can be asked any free-form question.

It helps solving concrete challenges when using it from Solidity, like string format and size of a question, as well as inverting the flow of control for the smart contract programmer.

RealityKeys has positioned itself for a different function: before the fact, they publish two public keys for any interesting event that can be decided as yes/no. One is for the no-case, one for the yes-case. These keys can be used to encrypt things, or verify signatures. After the event happened, RealityKeys publishes the private key for the actual outcome. E.g., the private yes-key if the event happened. And they promise that they destroy the other private key in that moment, for it never to see the light of day.

What you get from that is that you can pre-encrypt two things, one of which will never get known. Or, you can later sign one of two pre-arranged transactions, utilizing the private yes- or no-keys, as they become available. Which is exactly what you need to resolve a smart contract that is pre-programmed for an unknown outcome.

Oracle services will be a huge market.

It's safe to predict that the big rating agencies and information providers will offer paid oracle services directly into the blockchain world.

This is simple to do, will be an awesome, cheap and scaling source of revenue and kick financial dealings on the blockchain into overdrive.

There is no limit really for the complexity of financial products that can be realized on the blockchain, safe, and with guaranteed payout, often tied directly into other digital assets. These assets will be CDOs of a new generation: they will not only legally be a slice of the underlying collateral but tapping directly into the money.

Even a bet *in* Ether *on* the Ether price needs an oracle though. You need to be able to learn about the current rate somehow. That is not part of Ethereum. The price has to be learned from outside somehow even if everything else is about intrinsic parts of the blockchain.

Trustworthy oracles from established brands will make anything possible.

What is Timestamping?

Timestamping is something one gets for free with blockchain data. It is the main attraction for some use-cases.

The topic is relevant because current marketing efforts cause a bit of confusion and sometimes timestamping services are called blockchains now.

They clearly are not, if they don't also satisfy some other criteria, notably smart contracts.

Timestamps are something very useful, in essence they function as notaries and hand out a certificate that vouches for the fact that a certain data set looked a certain way at a given time.

For this, timestamping services would usually hash the data and publish the hash widely or put it somewhere so that at a later point it can be proven that the hash existed at that point in time. If the hash existed, the data must have existed, too, because it is unfeasible to store the hash first and then later come up with convenient data that matches it.

A good place to store the hash, of course, is a blockchain. A hash stored into it cannot be altered later. Because the block the hash was stored into can't. The hash itself is being treated as a piece of data, it is not in any way related to the block hash – except that it is becoming part of what is hashed to get the blockhash.

When using a blockchain, the timestamp is somewhat blurry though, which does not satisfy requirements of fintech in all cases. The actual time assigned to a block goes by the network time, which is the median time of what the individual nodes consider to be correct. But a blockchain can reliably number blocks and give order to transactions and for many applications that is good enough: to have a confirmed order.

There are also centralized services that require one to trust their word and their database, e.g. the system protection service Guardtime.[108] They can take on a different workload and operate in a different trust architecture, which requires you to trust them more than even your firewall vendor. Those are really ledgers and not about smart contracts.

A timestamping service can be built on top of any existing database, giving it a capability reminding of blockchains but still being much faster and having much higher capacity. *BigChainDB*[109] is such a case, on which *IPDB*,[110] a public but controlled ledger, is being built. *Ascribe*,[111] the creators of IPDB, describe it as global database for everyone, and as a *blockchain database* rather than a blockchain.

The relevant distinction is that a timestamp is never interacting with another timestamp the way accounts on a

108 Guardtime – https://guardtime.com
109 BigChainDB – https://www.bigchaindb.com
110 IPDB – https://ipdb.foundation
111 https://www.ascribe.io/

blockchain interact with each other. A timestamp can be compared to another but there is never a transfer between them, the are completely independent. And, therefore a lot of overhead can be abolished that is essential for a real blockchain to guarantee that transactions between two accounts are 'atomic', i.e. either change both accounts, or, when aborted, neither.

What is a Private Chain?

Your own walled-off garden.

A private chain[112] is a blockchain that is *not* open for everyone to be a miner or a validator.

It may well be opened up for anyone to come and make transactions on it. But the sign up will usually entail a registration process where real-world identity will be verified. This is not a must but lies in the nature of what private chains are being set up for.

Those standing up the chain – i.e. running the nodes – would have full control over who they allow in as transactors and what transactions can be executed by whom.

The miners, or validators, of a private chain are the folks who actually control it and they might often be an industry consortium, like the banks with R3 CEV. But it could be any industry really, shipping companies, IoT device manufacturers or energy utilities.

---

112 Vitalik on private chains: https://blog.ethereum.org/2015/08/07/on-public-and-private-blockchains/

Private chains use the exact same code.

To create a private Ethereum blockchain, you use the exact same client code that is used for the Ethereum mainnet and testnet. You just add a different genesis block and optionally choose a different network number.

For a private Bitcoin blockchain, minimal modifications suffice.

Many projects are private-chain only.

Hyperledger and Corda were designed for private chains from the start and don't even provide for the defenses that Bitcoin and Ethereum have built in to survive 'in the wild' as a public chain.

Miners become 'validators'.

The miners are not necessarily miners for a private chain, because the network is protected in a different way and incentives to operate the network are clear and rooted in off–chain, real–world agreements so that a mining reward and transaction fees don't make as much sense.

Instead, miners are usually called *validators*, as this is their main remaining function, they validate the proposed blocks coming to the chain. Ideally, every member of a consortium standing up the private chain operates one validator.

Consensus is easier for private chains.

In the simplest case, private chains could be stood up by so few validators, that a traditional, fault tolerant consensus protocol could be used. Those protocols are limited to less than a hundred validators (see pg. 225) but that should work with a small enough consortium where every participant operates one validator.

Or, as is the case now in other structures like SWIFT, only the bigger members of a consortium would operate validators and the smaller members would be content to only double check the data on the blockchain without direct technical power to *act* when an error or collusion is detected.

The alarms and reconciliation would be left to the traditional means of the real–world institutions – e.g. law –, which for established businesses is a perfectly fair approach.

Private chains can offer full finality.

Private chains that use traditional, fault tolerant consensus protocols can offer true finality instead of only probabilistic finality (pg. 229). This makes them very interesting for hard core financial applications.

This does not apply for private chains created using the current Ethereum or Bitcoin clients that use proof–of–work. A private chain based on them will only have probabilistic finality.

Private chains can be magnitudes faster.

A private chain that employs traditional, fault tolerant consensus protocols can be way faster and have a much higher capacity than public chains. The attainable performance will be close to normal databases.

As opposed to public chains that strive to be inclusive, private chains could simply require demanding hardware specs from their validators, including super fast network connections.

Once parallel transaction processing has been solved, a private chain consisting of z^{113} mainframe validators should be quite a sight to see. This might be a way to scale performance up and get challenging use cases for blockchains covered first. Not least because of the number of light clients that could connect to a z full client.

Private chains have their own token.

Private chains don't have the real Ether, they inherit their own token from the Ethereum source code of course, so it looks and quacks exactly like the original Ether.

But having your own currency is not what private chains are about. It's just a side–effect.

Private chains are cheaper and safer.

Ethereum transactions are not exactly cheap at the current price of Ether and to make the mainnet safer against attacks, the price to execute transactions has just been increased. We calculated it through at IBM, you can't really use the mainnet for IoT at this point, running decentralized code on it is just too expensive.

But with your private, free Ether, if you make a mistake, you are on the safe side. In so far as attackers can even access your private chain, they can still not steal any real cryptocurrency.

---

113 IBM z13   http://www-03.ibm.com/systems/z/hardware/z13.html

Private chains lose interoperability.

Of course, the promise of the 'world computer' is lost for a private chain, unless ways are found in the future to create safe networks between private chains.

The charm of Ethereum is that systems could inter-operate – by sharing the mainnet – that were created without knowledge of each other. Ultimately, Ether is the means to drive such interactions. Private chains do not have direct access to Ether, nor to the plethora of systems we are hoping to see on the mainnet.

The fact that anyone can safely use any smart contract deployed to the public blockchain is a promise of huge productivity gains and a receipt for the joint creation of massively complex systems.

Ethereum is a bit overkill for a private chain.

Obviously, Ethereum has all the necessary defenses built in to survive as public chain. Not only did a lot of engineering go into building these defenses but they also cost a price during operation. So a well engineered system, designed for use in a private network should become the technology of choice, as soon as that becomes available. Because it doesn't pay these overhead costs.

However, so far, Ethereum is still the best choice for many private scenarios. Simply by virtue of working, having some battle testing under its belt and building out a pool of developers to draw from.

What is the EVM?

For the remainder of this section, we are getting Ethereum–specific. The *EVM*, *Gas* and *Solidity* exist only in Ethereum. But they are so essential that any future competition to Ethereum will have to implement something alike. In this regard, Ethereum has extended what it means to be a blockchain, beyond what Bitcoin pioneered.

Bitcoin and Ethereum have a *virtual machine*.

Both systems define transactions as scripts, not a mere set of parameters. That script is executed to perform the actual 'transacting'. A transaction coming to the blockchain is expected to be a list of instructions, a *bytecode*, that is then executed, step–by–step, by the respective *virtual machine*.

The Bitcoin virtual machine does not have its own name. Ethereum's virtual machine is known as EVM.

A virtual machine executes programs.

The Java virtual machine (JVM) is probably the best known example of a virtual machine.

It was invented for the Internet of Things (IoT) to make programs more robust and more portable than when written in C. At one point, a virtual machine that executed Java bytecode was powering all cell phones that were using Android, which is written in Java.

A C++ *compiler* compiles C++ programs to machine code that a specific processor can understand and execute. A program has to be compiled separately for each different type of hardware.

Java programs are compiled *not* to machine code but to an intermediary form instead, called bytecode, that is made to be executed by the virtual machine that understands it. The bytecode is independent of any specific hardware.

When a Java program is executed, what that really means is that a Java Runtime program is started, which contains the JVM, which is fed the bytecode to run.

The bytecode instructions are evaluated step by step and the JVM is performing the expected tasks as laid out in the bytecode. The JVM itself is understood by the hardware processors because it *is* written in machine code.

The individual instructions of the bytecode are also called *opcodes*.

A virtual machine is more robust and more portable but not as fast.

Using a VM incurs a significant performance penalty, because the way the VM executes bytecode is more complex than when a hardware processor executes machine code directly.

The advantage is that a program that consists of byte-code is portable across different machines. As long as a Java Runtime exists on a certain machine, one can execute a Java program on it, no matter where and how it was compiled. One does not have to know the target hardware at compile time, as with C++. And the program needs to be compiled only once, not separately for every target hardware type.

Programs that use virtual machines to execute are also more robust, because the virtual machine can perform checks during execution to avert the worst types of crashes. This advantage enabled Java to break into the corporate IT landscape that was dominated by C++.

Ethereum has 4 compilers and 8 runtimes.

Ethereum smart contract scripts are stored on the blockchain in bytecode – EVM opcodes – and executed by the EVM. Like with the Java Virtual Machine, an EVM executes the opcodes that were compiled by a compiler.

The opcodes were defined in the Yellow Paper and there is only this one definition of them.

But smart contracts can be *written* in four different languages, each featuring its own compiler. And they can be *executed* by any of the eight different Ethereum client implementations, which all contain an EVM.

The four languages are: *Solidity*, *Serpent*, *LLL* and *Mutan*. These are all languages invented specifically for Ethereum but inspired by JavaScript, Python, *Lisp*[114] and Go respectively. And as mentioned, Ethereum clients have in turn been written in Python, C++, Go, Javascript, Java,

---

114 Lisp is one of the oldest programming languages around and was developed as a list processing language for Artificial Intelligence.

Haskell, Ruby and Rust. They all implement the EVM as essential part of the client.

The EVM opcodes are the common denominator of all these languages and clients. They are what is stored on the blockchain and what 'Ethereum' – i.e. the EVM – really understands.

The EVM is what executes the transactions, distributed code, smart contracts and Dapps.

The EVM executes the opcodes one-by-one. They are like very low level language elements and can be visualized as a very primitive programming language. They can also be written directly by hand, without using a compiler. In rare cases there is use for that, too.

But since most programs on the blockchain were created by the Solidity compiler, the actual opcode programs on the chain reflect optimizations and overhead that this compiler adds and are not a straight forward read. Still, they are stored on the blockchain without protection for everyone to inspect at any time. And they are signed by whoever deployed them as part of the deployment process.

One can also write opcodes directly into Solidity programs, bypassing the Solidity compiler. Because this resembles embedding machine language instructions into C programs, the opcodes are then dubbed 'assembler'.

No competition.

There is no other relevant virtual machine out there currently, to program real smart contracts in.

> # The EVM is the
> # industry standard.

Ethereum, Eris, Tendermint and Rootstock all use the EVM. Hyperledger is looking into utilizing it. Dfinity will use it. Eris had forked it but is hurrying to get back to using the original one.

The Bitcoin VM is just very limited in its capabilities and doesn't even have or need a high language compiler.

Of course the unique position of the EVM will be challenged but the Ethereum developers are working to keep the advantage. A faster EVM, closer to the bare metal is in the works, somewhere in an old school bus in rural Indiana.

The EVM was built for monetary transactions.

It has since been cranked up to go beyond financial transactions to support general purpose programming. Due to its more humble origins, programmers now face some severe restrictions.

E.g. the use of strings – meaning, any text, anything not a number or a list – is limited beyond painful. One of the most problematic challenge this incurs is the assembly of URLs to query external services – oracles – in a meaningful way.

Another very hard limit, restrictions in local registers, sits a bit deeper and Solidity shields the programmer from it in valiant manner. However, the hoops it has to go through are a result of how things were blown up beyond the original purpose on the way.

With the arrival of Martin Becze's new VM design, *eWASM,* this may change radically for Ethereum 2.0.

Smart contract execution can be handled off-chain.

A VM is not the only way that smart contracts can be executed.

One can store any data into the chain, also opcodes of any other virtual machine, e.g. Java's. These opcodes can then be executed by a system that the Ethereum system is completely agnostic about.

The node synchronization of the blockchain can still be exploited and a parallel world state and consensus can be maintained by all nodes that interpret the data the same way. This approach is called *color coins*[115] as it resembles marking coins: it doesn't change them but you can tell them apart now, potentially for other purposes than payment.

This is how the Bitcoin blockchain can be used for more powerful scripts that go beyond the capabilities that are built into the Bitcoin VM and how other products, e.g. Corda want to roll.

The project that Vitalik and *Yanislav Malahov* worked on when they first discussed a basic idea for Ethereum, was also based on the principle to store things into the blockchain that its VM is agnostic about.

---

115 More on color coins on pg. 277.

Determinism is a sufficient reason to define and implement a dedicated VM.

Ripple's ambitious Codius project sought to add smart contracts to Ripple in the way just described. They ran up hard against the challenges one encounters when trying to re-use existing language compilers and VMs.

One major problem is to ensure that a program arrives at the same result on thousands of machines. This can only happen when the execution environment can guarantee *determinism*. Which means that given the same input a program will always arrive at the same result.

VMs of existing languages, say, Go, do not guarantee that at all. They liberally interoperate with pseudo random generators, time or periphal devices that can make any program execution result differ ever so slightlty from that of the same program on the next computer.

The EVM 2.0 plans.

The Codius experience, however, inspired WASM, which is now used for a stab at the next generation of the EVM. WASM is developed by Mozilla, Google and Microsoft and stands for Web Assembly. It's first ambition is to safely run machine code in the browser, which could make dynamic web pages a lot faster. For the EVM, the research likewise has the goal to run EVM opcodes as native machines codes of a computer's CPU.

This would also allow to use existing libraries, written in other languages. They would be compiled into WASM and from there made available to decentralized code written in any language that can be compiled to WASM.

What is Gas?

Gas addresses the Halting Problem.

What if you wrote a buggy contract that has an infinite loop? And remember that every contract script is run on all nodes of the network. So a proper infinite loop would stall *all* nodes of the network.

The short answer is, *it will run out of gas.*

This is called metering and it's how you are prevented from bringing thousands of nodes down with one typo. And then the transaction will be rolled back as if nothing had happened.

This protects not only against honest mistakes but likewise against attacks on the network as a whole.

To this end, every Ethereum transaction must get a maximum cost assigned by the transactor. When that maximum is hit during execution, which can only be found out by trying to execute it, the transaction is aborted and rolled back – but the maximum cost is still incurred.

Triggering those maxima unknowingly is a main point of frustration for new Ethereum programmers. Your code costs, by the instruction. You have to supply it with cryptocurrency to run. It's different.

Transactions use gas to run.

Gas is used to calculate the cost of transactions in Ether. Gas is not the same as Ether. Eventually, the cost is paid to the miners in Ether. But along the way it is called gas. And how much one unit of gas costs in Ether is calculated rather late in the game:

So – every single *operation* of a contract instance costs the initiator of the transaction a certain, *fix* amount of *gas*. The underlying system really counts beans.

The cost is incurred *not* to the creator of the contract instance, but the *caller* who calls a method of a contract instance. Though when you *create* a contract instance, this is a transaction itself and does cost you gas, lots of it.

But if someone else later makes a call to it, all costs are theirs. When you make a call to it yourself, obviously, you pay. This is a crucial design factor for systems on Ethereum.

The *gas cost* is a fix value per lowest level operation, i.e. per *opcode* of the virtual machine. E.g. 1 gas for every 32 bit when expanding memory, 20 gas for the calculation of a hash etc.

The sum of the gas cost of all operations *executed* during a *transaction* is the transaction's gas cost. Not the sum of the cost of all operations that the *contract* source *has* that the transaction might be calling into. But what operations actually got executed.

Which means a loop can get very expensive. But on the other hand a simple call to a large contract can be very low cost.

E.g. 21,000 gas is a base cost for every transaction, and 5 gas for every byte of data or code it is parametrized with. Except only 1 for zero bytes (a hack). And so on.

The total transaction gas cost is then multiplied with the *gas price*, e.g. currently 0.00001 Ether to arrive at the *transaction cost* in Ether.

So in all: the *gas cost* is a fix figure per *operation*. The *sum* of which are multiplied with the *gas price*. The result is the *transaction cost* in Ether.

All this goes on behind the scenes, the logic being embedded deep in the bowels of the virtual machine.

Gas is paid in Ether, to miners.

As mentioned, this is the official raison d'etre for Ether.

Now it gets confusing. The effective price of gas in Ether fluctuates and is technically a proposal by someone wanting to execute a transaction, to the miners to put them into the blockchain.

Miners are free to ignore transactions that they feel offer too low a gas price.

In practice, for now, everyone on the mainnet offers the same gas price, e.g. 10 szabo per 1 gas, which is 0.00001 Ether, or at some point in 2016 USD 0.00000226255.

People could even go lower because there are way less transactions to be executed currently than space for transactions in blocks. Many blocks are empty these days.

But this is meant to work in the future as a mechanism of supply and demand:

if at some point there are more transactions to be handled then the network has capacity, then the gas price, offered as per transaction, will determine whether a transaction will be executed soon, later or – never at all.

Transactions are *not* guaranteed to make it into the blockchain.

There are other reasons for it but having offered too little pay for it is the most important one.

The way things work in Bitcoin and Ethereum, many miners try and propose a block at every given time but only one block gets accepted eventually and so only one miner collects all the rewards and transaction fees for that round. You can find the opinion that it might have been a bad idea to reward only one lucky miner per round.

It's also a fact that every full node in the network has to execute every transaction and they should all get some reward, too.

But the basic principle for rewarding nodes that sustain the network is that everyone gets to mine a block now and then and then collects all the rewards for their efforts in the form of mining and transaction fees at that point. Statistically that should play out. In practice, it works a bit differently in Bitcoin today and Ethereum might have to fine-tune its incentives one day, too.

Gas *might* be a dead end.

Gas is a major invention of Ethereum but might still go away.

It fails the plausibility check of elegance as a solution to a core problem. Which proves nothing. Gas prices also played an unlucky role in recent attacks were imbalances between the price tags of operations were exploited.

But more importantly one of gas' main functions, solving the Halting Problem, might be overcome in different ways.

Since programs executed on the blockchain are too slow at this point to hold all business logic of a medium complex system, then if the core business logic is programmed off-chain, only calling into the blockchain for key state changes, those scripts on the chain may neither need loops, nor gotos, nor have to call each other.

As a result, they would *not* have to be Turing-complete and be certain to end at some point and not have a Halting Problem. They could not have infinite loops. They would not have to have the safety latch of running out of gas.

This would be a RISC[116]–like development for blockchain code that could be expected as next step after getting as versatile as possible, thus maybe for Ethereum 3.0.

And this does not discount the other good reason for gas, to be a billing mechanism for using other people's computers to execute your decentralized code.

However, if only that is left, given how indirect and uneven the distribution of the miner fees is at any rate, this could turn out to not be a sufficient argument.

An alternate approach to gas might be to add a sophisticated *type system* to Ethereum.

Type systems have since long been used to detect errors before a program even starts — e.g. when it is compiled to machine readable code. They could allow us to both reason about a smart contract's correctness and do away with the danger of infinite loops.

---

116 Reduced instruction set computing, an 80's CPU design strategy offering a smaller choice, of less powerful instructions that execute faster than the more complex instructions of 60's CPU designs.

What is Solidity?

Solidity is the main language for programming Ethereum.

It is a Javascript-like, general purpose language designed for programming decentralized applications, but also the best compensation for some deficiencies of the Ethereum virtual machine.

Usually if anyone today talks about programming in Ethereum, they will implicitly mean, programming Solidity. All our examples were shown in Solidity.

The Ecosystem springing up around Ethereum is almost exclusively geared towards Solidity and it's the most sophisticated compiler for Ethereum.

Solidity is not what the Ethereum virtual machine executes in the end. Those are the EVM opcodes as explained above. Solidity source is compiled to those opcodes. The advanced, complex syntax of Solidity is condensed into that straight forward, primitive instruction set that is optimal for being executed by a VM.

Solidity was planned to have strong testing gears.

The original reason to create a new language was to create a complete programming environment that would allow for more powerful tests. Writing distributed programs has unique challenges and some things are ridiculously hard to test, let alone write automated tests for.

The idea was to built the tools for this right into the compiler and this is still sorely needed. At this point it has not materialized yet but the attacks of autumn 2016 gave it new urgency.

There are four other languages.

Of the other languages created throughout the last two years, only one is still in use: Vitalik still makes important new proposals in his language *Serpent*,[117] which is reminiscent of Python. The Ethereum–based prediction market *Augur*[118] reports they are preferring it.

Because Vitalik also leads the Foundation's research on proof–of–stake and scalability, there is a chance that cutting-edge extensions to play with these features will first pop up in Serpent.

Monax liked using the lisp-like LLL when they started out with Eris but are now basing their contract framework on Solidity. LLL won a new lease on life, however, when the core of the very important effort to give Ethereum a *name service* was ported from Solidity to LLL in a bid to make the code more secure and faster. Because LLL can be easier to review and the compiler produces less opcode

---

117 Serpent tutorial   https://github.com/ethereum/wiki/wiki/Serpent
118 Augur – https://www.augur.net

compared to Solidity. This has lead to bold calls for LLL's 'ressurection'[119] on the grounds that smart contracts are hard at any rate.

Mutan was inspired by Go and officially retired for the quite similar looking Solidity.

They all have the fifth language in common, which they all compile to, the Ethereum VM opcodes. As common denominator, the VM opcodes make it possible that any program coming from any of the four different languages can be mixed with programs written in any other language, and run at the same time. Because on the blockchain, it's all just opcodes anyway.

Note that opcode lists that are the result of different language compilers (e.g. Serpent vs. Solidity), constituting programs *doing* the same in any of the four higher languages will not *look* too similar, as each language has its own specific overhead and implicit structures that reflect the opcode generation process and shape the resulting opcode list.

---

119 LLL ressurection   http://blog.syrinx.net/the-resurrection-of-lll-part-1

CAVEATS

"Arrgh."

Egan Ford

How Fast is Ethereum (Latency)?

Latency is the time that you have to wait until an operation is complete.

Super fast to sort–of finality.

A blockchain transfer is
very fast to *finality*.

It's around 1,000 times faster than stock exchanges settle and 100,000 times faster than credit card payments.

Finality means that a transaction is complete and cannot be stopped or reverted anymore. It's after a trade has been cleared and settled, or a credit card charge is past its chargeback time window.

The finality that Ethereum offers is of a slightly weaker nature, as discussed above, with fewer guarantees than expected from a normal database. Or payment system.

The rhythm of transaction handling in blockchains is governed by the *blocktime*, which in Bitcoin is about 10 minutes, in Ethereum, about 17 seconds. The blocktime determines how fast an issued transaction should be considered to 'have happened'.

Because the finality for blockchains using proof–of–work is probabilistic (see pg. 229), rather than having a clear threshold for it, a transaction gets successively more likely to be committed over time.

The accepted rule of thumb for this is:

An Ethereum transaction is considered final after twelve blocks.

So after blocktime times twelve – about three minutes – a transactions is deemed to be final. The twelve is pretty arbitrary and resembles the security that six blocks give you with Bitcoin. Although the Bitcoin mainnet is still much safer as it has a much higher hash rate.

Completing a trade at an exchange takes three days. In comparison to that, blockchains are super fast, it's a huge advantage they offer and that's why the major exchanges the world over are looking into it: Nasdaq, NYSE, CME, TMX, LSE, Deutsche Börse, JPX, ASX, DMCC, KRX.

For a credit card payment to actually be final, it takes about two to four months. Merchants are used to living with that and for the shopping experience, the only latency that matters is how fast the *proposal* to send the money to the merchant is approved, which takes mere seconds.

For Bitcoin and Ethereum the equivalent is the moment a transaction is *broadcast* to the network, which equally only takes seconds. And that's all you wait for when paying for the best burgers in Berlin at room77.[120]

And Jörg really has the money a minute later. Rather than a couple of months.

These *months* shorter wait times and often hugely lower, fix fees do make a difference for small shops.

Writes are very slow.

But the blocktime is the same for any simple write to the blockchain. This is an essential factor e.g. for blockchain programs for IoT. And that's painfully slow.

> Blockchains commit state
> *very* slowly.

We are talking about three minutes here for one confirmed, certain write for Ethereum, versus *milliseconds* for free databases like *mySQL*[121] or *VoltDB*.[122] That's four to five magnitudes. If you have a bad day with Amazon's database cloud service, you'll still be three magnitudes faster per write.

This has dire consequences. In IoT, you don't want users to wait for anything for more than about a minute, which means that at this point you can only make *one write*

---

120 room77 is accepting bitcoin for burgers since 2011 – http://room77.de
121 MySQL is the most popular Open Source database.
122 VoltDB is the fastest – https://www.voltdb.com

to the blockchain during any meaningful action, e.g. device registration, which is hugely limiting.

What is Ethereum's Capacity (Throughput)?

Throughput means how many transactions you can do in parallel. It is expressed in transactions per second (tps).

While one Ethereum transaction will take three minutes to finalize – that's its latency –, about 100 to 200 transactions can be handled in parallel during that time.

Ethereum can do around 10 transactions per second.

Like – globally. That is a laughably low capacity. Bitcoin is in the same ballpark.

> ## Blockchains have a *very* small capacity.

Visa is said to be handling 2,000 tps, on average, with peaks of 40,000+. A *VoltDB* cluster – an ultra high-throughput database – can handle more than 1,000,000 tps. Blockchains cannot compete with this. IPDB is getting there but does not have Ethereum's features. It is made for storage, not transactions, nor does it allow for smart contracts.

Adding insult to injury, the VoltDB transactions are fully *ACID*[123], rather than *eventually consistent,*[124] or *probabilistically final* (see pg. 229). That's how many worlds apart Ethereum is from modern databases.

But – those databases *don't move money*. Per design, Visa transactions also do *not* directly move money. They are recommendations and requests. And that makes a huge difference. Ethereum transfers are of an altogether different quality.

You could simply run many chains in parallel to increase the capacity of your system. This is at the heart of the future designs being in the works now. But that doesn't change the fact that the capacity of an individual blockchain network is at this point toy-like. Running multiple chains as they come now, won't allow for transferring anything between the chains.

This will improve.

Ethereum improved on the consensus protocol that Bitcoin uses to reach its faster blocktime and we can expect further significant improvement.

Bitcoin core devs are fighting very bruising and public battles over how to improve Bitcoin's limits and there are ways. They fight with code, which is good and the way it

---

123 A set of attributes that you intuitively expect from a database. Basically that what you write to it will be what you read back from it.

124 Also called *BASE*, a weaker guarantee than ACID that promises only that at some point in the future you will read what you wrote. In the mean time it could be an old value or somebody else's update.

should be. People don't just talk, they show working proposals.

But it is still tearing the community apart, and this in–
fighting was behind the mid 2016 article about Bitcoin's
'failure' on the NYT cover. Of course, the interviewee's
employer, R3, was also just about to launch a product in
the space. And understandably, given Bitcoin's colorful
past, R3 and the big banks in its consortium cannot be
seen as Bitcoin lovers.

Still the fact remains that Bitcoin was simply not, at all,
ever, designed to handle the massive amounts of transactions you'd need to handle world commerce, or even 'only'
what Visa handles every day.

It was obviously not designed giving much of a damn
about huge numbers of people using it, or even using it
over a long time! Your hard disk would just spill over.
Maybe the creators hoped the shortfalls would be figured
out over time. They'd be half-right.

The Ethereum devs had scalability on their minds from
day one. The internal layout of Ethereum's data model is
prepared to work with a much larger network. It's debatable whether the core ideas were strong choices, there was
not much big data experience involved and quite some
undue love for complex and novel solutions.

Plus, since the task of scaling was found to be quite
demanding, it had to be deferred to a later release. Today
there is more than one opinion among the core people,
how performance and scale should be approached.

The Ethereum Foundation's approach for *sharding*, lead
by Vitalik aims at increasing Ethereum's capacity 80-fold
as a start.

Why *do* blockchains have such a low capacity?

Because, as mentioned before, *every transaction is calculated in parallel*, the *same way*, on every computer in the network.

This is not a design for capacity or speed – in fact, it's the opposite. And this is not even counting in the effort required for *consensus*: i.e. making sure everyone will agree with everyone else's results.

As opposed to that, modern databases, and certainly the internal design of Visa's system, distribute work so that multiple *different* groups of transactions are handled in parallel across a big cluster of computers. This is what the term *parallel processing* usually means and it makes things much, much faster and increases throughput. Google's search response times are a prime example.

It's not always easy to distribute work into chunks that can be handled in parallel. Those chunks cannot interact and cannot manipulate the same state. That is the main challenge for distributed database design.

Blockchains don't even try.

It's a tough proposition for blockchains, too, because cryptocurrency transactions can often access the same state. Still, achieving some parallelism with transaction handling is being developed for Ethereum right now. It's an obvious optimization.

Another factor for the low throughput is that blockchains operate across large networks of thousands of nodes, around 5,000 for Bitcoin[125] and around 7,500 for

125 Bitcoin node count: https://bitnodes.21.co/

Ethereum.[126] And, to be as *safe* as possible, it is desirable for a blockchain to have as many nodes as possible.

For one, it takes a different kind of algorithm to find consensus among so many nodes, than what is used for traditional database clusters, which usually only have tens of nodes, at a maximum. And this algorithm slows things down.

Secondly, the transaction data needs to be ferried around so that all nodes can verify every transaction. With a big set of nodes, this simply takes some time.

Blockchain networks are super large.

The way that blockchains keep thousands of computers in sync is novel, super fast, low-overhead and – based on game theory.

The algorithms used to synchronize nodes in traditional distributed systems, such as *Paxos* or *Practical Byzantine Fault Tolerance* (PBFT)[127] would simply stop working when applied to a cluster with thousands of nodes. Those systems negotiate a consensus *before* each transaction. All nodes, in a chatty way, make sure that they will remain in sync, before they make any state change. Failing that, e.g. if too many nodes don't answer in time, they don't progress at all.

But beyond roughly 100 nodes – Hyperledger is shooting for 64 –, one can't afford to have every node talk with every other node for every state change. Because the effort for this communication grows quadratically with the number of nodes. Faster hardware will only alleviate that

---

126 Ethereum node count: https://www.ethernodes.org/network/1

127 PBFT – http://pmg.csail.mit.edu/papers/osdi99.pdf

so much. This effect will forever outpace Moore's Law[128], which is becoming toothless at any rate.

Therefore, today's blockchains that are based on proof–of–work, just share *results*, and their secret sauce is how they have *no need for a synchronization step*. And that is new.

But still, instead of splitting work up, then combining results – as in Google's awed *map-reduce* algorithm – everything is calculated by everyone. And often times, multiple competing results that differ only in window dressing but have the same actual contents are sent around for the participants in the network to decide, each for themselves, which one to accept as new truth.

Private chains can excel at speed.

If, however, a very small number of nodes is acceptable, e.g. for a private network (cf. pg. 194), this can be used for a massive performance boost by using some form of proof–of–stake or PBFT and/or by requiring very powerful machines for the validators.

Hydrachain[129] is the experimental Ethereum variant that implements PBFT.

State Channels can solve the problem.

Raiden[130] is being developed by Heiko Hees' men to address the throughput and latency challenges of Ethereum. It could make things maximally performant, on par

---

128 The observation by Gordon Moore, co-founder of Intel, that computer hardware is becoming doubly as powerful about every 1 ½ years.

129 Hydrachain – https://github.com/HydraChain/hydrachain

130 Raiden are state channels for Ethereum – http://raiden.network

with legacy technology. And in fact one bank dev joked that state channels are what banks use since the 70's.

Raiden is a *state channel* concept inspired by Bitcoin's *Lightning Network*[131]. The difference is that Raiden will be compatible with Ethereum without a change to Ethereum. The same is not true for the Lightning Network, which would a require significant update to Bitcoin to be able to 'hook into it.'

This is a direct benefit of Ethereum's greater programmability, exactly what it was made for. And therefore, state channels are expected to become a reality for Ethereum first, because a change to Bitcoin is a difficult proposition.

State channels are pure *peer-to-peer*: they establish a direct connection between two parties who often deal with each other and collect large numbers of transactions before settling them on the blockchain. They require bonds on the blockchain and each state channel transaction is basically a small, digitally signed cheque secured by the bond. In the end the 'cheques' are settled using the bond and releasing the rest of it back to the payee.

The settling costs only one blockchain transaction and there is no practical limit as to how many 'cheques' can be piled up and cleared in one go. The method can even be optimized in such a way that the blockchain is never used at all, except to settle a dispute. A smart contract on the blockchain then acts as automatic judge over the fate of the bond, inspecting the state channel micro transactions presented to it.

This judge could be expected to be consistently predictable and fair, which would eliminate any incentive to ever call on it. The parties will always know that they can settle for free using the site channels, or for a small fee for

131 Lightning Network by Joseph Poon – https://lightning.network

arbitration on the blockchain. (Almost) any incentive to cheat would be eliminated – and that would allow the blockchain to support innumerous state channels because they would put almost no work load on it beyond placing bonds. Which could be left untouched and recycled forever.

But there are fringe cases about the state channel approach that still have to be figured out. *Jeff Coleman*[132] of *LedgerLabs*[133] is currently working on a general framework to support the entire range of possible Ethereum state channels.

---

132 Jeff Coleman – https://twitter.com/technocrypto
133 LedgerLabs – https://ledgerlabs.com

What is Probabilistic Finality?

The scale and speed of blockchains comes at a high price: strict *finality* is sacrificed for it. This means that it is not certain that the result of a transaction will be permanent. It can disappear.

To learn about any part of the state of a blockchain, e.g. the balance of an account, you ask a node.

But it's never quite clear whether a node really has it right and its information might always still change, dramatically. Because nodes can at any time change their minds about the world state – and they do that as soon as they sense that a different view will prevail. Essentially, because they find out that more nodes, or more powerful nodes, seem to believe that other truth. This is true for any blockchain using proof–of–work consensus.

Because the game theoretical pressure of that algorithm is *not* so much giving incentive for a node to hold a *consistent* world view, but rather to make nodes compromise and come to a *common* view. And those become mutually exclusive goals whenever groups of nodes get severed from the rest. When the network is 'partitioned', or 'forked' into two different opinions about the official world state.

That's why a node can never be certain that its estimate about the world state is correct – say, about how much Ether an account holds – and the information it gives can therefore, by definition, never be considered 100% reliable.

One could say that weeks old transactions and their results are, for all intents and purposes, as good as final. But there could be fringe cases, you'd really have to look at the development of the network size – more exactly: the total hash rate – over the past days to be all certain.

All this is of course massively incompatible with many financial applications. It can be surprisingly ok though for many other applications, e.g. in IoT.

So proof–of–work blockchain nodes can ever only give a highly *likely* information about what's a fact, which at some point, is regarded as virtual certainty. And this is what is called *probabilistic finality*.

It is a pragmatic view to say that finality of a transaction is achieved as soon as twelve blocks have been processed after the one your transaction was in. But it is doubly misleading.

It will almost always be true. But there is no guarantee as it does not account for forks that can happen, bugs or attacks that could split the networks for hours or days.

Now this is actually true for the traditional payment networks. They could also have bugs. In fact they do have outages. But they do not move money. They don't claim to be final.

On the other hand, with the traditional consensus methods that we had before blockchains, a result *is always* final, once a majority of nodes agreed upon it. Those mechanisms are not immune to network partitions either though. If too many nodes are lost, such network just stops processing.

And they work well only somewhere below a hundred nodes, which is not an option for public blockchain networks.

So at this point in time, one has to choose between strict finality + speed, and availability + scale.

How Ready is Ethereum?

Ethereum comes with no warranties.

That big disclaimer on the Ethereum web page, to not use it for any serious business, is now gone.

But even with version 1.0 now officially reached, there will never be any warranties made for Ethereum – unless a big company gets behind it one day. As an Open Source project, Ethereum proper will always carry the disclaimer that it comes *as-is*, with no warranties of any kind.

This is true for much essential software though, like Linux or Apache. And they are still used by very security conscious companies.

People are right now working hard to make Ethereum as robust and unbreakable as possible. IBM is running global networks bigger and with much more load than the mainnet, helping to harden it. Mid 2016 we had seen the frequency of finding significant errors in the Go client drop from roughly every two weeks to every two months. But then came a spate of attacks that revealed a host of problems, some of them rather hard to fix. It's hard to tell how many more of these are lurking.

IBM has in the past made sure that business customers can rely on Linux, or Java. When Microsoft acted on the thread that Linux posed to their business, IBM stepped in and gave a promise to indemnify its customers against the fallout: IBM basically guaranteed to take over any fees that could arise from Unix patent violations of the Linux Open Source programmers. And paid. Big time in the end, shielding its customers.

With Apache, many banks are not using the free, Open Source version, but IBM's for-pay version, *WebSphere*, that made IBM billions but therefore comes from a company a bank could sue – and that has deep enough pockets to pay – in case something went terribly wrong with their web servers. Finally, WebSphere has this strong focus on scaling workload out while keeping things easy for programmers.

These factors, fnancial protection from bugs, and industry-grade scalability are essential for making a product deployable by big corporations. There is a whole dimension of what makes a software be a product that the Ethereum team has relatively little interest in or know-how about. In that regard, there is no real effort to make Ethereum business-ready.

IBM specifically knows how to integrate products into the IT landscape of their customers. This is why Hyperledger draws excited praise. And the same IBM Fellow, Gennario Cuomo, who created WebSphere, has spearheaded the IBM blockchain efforts.

It's fair to say that the EVM is 80% of what Ethereum is. Since Hyperledger is now looking at the Ethereum Virtual Machine, to make it pluggable into Hyperledger, Ethereum may yet 'become Hyperledger', in a way. And unsurprisingly, because it does the core task best.

Ethereum is a protocol.

Another way to answer the question about readiness is that 'Ethereum' is a *protocol*, not any specific program, implementation or network. And that this protocol has worked almost flawlessly.

A protocol is the definition of how things should talk to each other. How they get in touch and how they react to misunderstandings. Of what zeros and ones coming over the wire are to mean what numbers and letters.

The protocol is not perfect. There are changes coming to make it more powerful. But it worked as expected at this point. A remarkable achievement.

Ethereum had a very good start.

Astoundingly few bugs popped up during beta[134] and pre-beta, which was very encouraging. The beta phase was ended faster than expected. Then again there was not much real load on the network ever. Even now, there is little business humming on mainnet.

And it is not quite clear what was tested: the protocol, or the clients. Because the clients are still buggy enough and are being heavily reworked, introducing quite a number of new errors on the way.

It took Bitcoin years to mature, with tens of glitches found during operation, some rather bad. Ethereum will have to be allowed some of the same public maturing. Not all features in it where cleanly designed from the start, there is much 'Gaffer taping', as Vitalik calls it.

---

134 The Beta version of a program usually has all features of the release version but is expected to still have some bugs.

But it is faring *much* better than most people – including most of the makers – expected.

Ethereum had a top-notch security audit.

The Ethereum team wisely spent six digits on security audits by bad ass professionals, who promptly turned around and launched their own Ethereum clone, cause that's how the world works.

But for the good money they also helped weeding out about a hundred bugs the Ethereum guys had not found themselves, some of them really nasty ones that would have bitten if encountered in the wild. Smart move all around really.

The clone is *Rootstock*. That Ethereum–on–top–of– Bitcoin project (see pg. 75).

Ethereum got some real flak, later.

The biggest threat to Ethereum's success materialized in the form of 'Ethereum Classic' after The DAO hard–fork. Arguably this was the result of taking a fix for an application to the platform level and damaging its standing and security in the process.

The second hard–fork that year was to fix a design weakness that was a rather sad case of over-engineering. A special case that had been introduced turned out to be a vulnerability and there is the opinion that there are just too many special cases in the protocol, that are not all thought through to the end, which, unwisely, broadened the attack-able surface area.

None of these problems would exist without the consistent effort of at least decently knowledgable hackers to bring the system down. The way they benefit might be from shorting Ether before running an attack. This means that they make money the moment the Ether exchange rate goes down due to the bad news.

All around, as helpful as the audit was, it did not check for systemic problems and as formal as the Yellow Paper tried to get, it was not its role to address implementation problems where the memory just runs over at some point or the disks run out of space from storing junk into the chain for zero fees. And maybe it didn't get the metering quite right for some special cases where contracts end themselves.

It's kind of ok that the product is maturing in the hands of the customers, it's what you are seeing every-where since decades now. It's just a little scary it's happening with 1 billion USD value on its chain. Then again, it took that sort of money to make it attractive enough for the attackers, which now 'help' hardening it.

The plan forward is clear: simplicity, scale and ecology.

There are very concrete plans and research going on for Ethereum 1.1, and 2.0. One finds the original research explained at the Ethereum blog. The most important of which are to reach scale and performance and to get rid of the electricity wasting proof–of–work consensus protocol that Ethereum inherited from Bitcoin.

There is also a strong commitment to make the imple-mentation of Ethereum simpler under the hood, which will make it easier to upgrade and extend it with custom programming – Vitalik's main design goal from inception.

How Difficult is Ethereum to Use?

Ethereum smart contracts would have to be programmed with the rigidity of Space Shuttle programs: they just can't be allowed fail. They should be flawless. Not only bug–free but proven to be so. Because once deployed, they cannot be changed.

That's a pretty long way from where we are now.

Formal verification.

One way to prove the correctness of a program, e.g. a smart contract, is the use of *formal verification*. That means using hard math to find a proof that a program does what it should. And especially, does not do what it should not do.

The Ethereum Foundation has hired a specialist who is inspecting the EVM and simple Ethereum contracts to look for ways to prove their correctness and bring formal verification to Ethereum.

This is a doable undertaking because at this point, Ethereum smart contracts have no concurrency, the EVM is a very simple virtual machine, contracts are relatively small programs and both the EVM opcode and Solidity are simple languages.

The challenge is to express what you are concretely trying to prove.

Solidity is also getting extended with an annotation syntax for *Why3*, allowing to reason about the correctness of individual smart contracts. This will look like in the shortened example below.

The first 'commented out' lines check at compile–time, before the code even runs, that all entries in `ledger` add up to the same `total` again everytime the contract has been executed.

```
/// ..
/// @why3 contract-account invariant {
/// @why3    sum #ledger = total
/// @why3 }
contract MyShares {
  mapping (address => uint256) ledger;
  function transfer(
    address sdr, address rcv, uint256 amt) {
    if (ledger[sdr] < amt) throw;
    ledger[sdr] -= amt;
    ledger[rcv] += amt;
  }
  ..
}
```

So this is like programming programs right into the programs to be tested. And that's the degree of security that smart contracts need. How much overhead smart contract code would need to make it tollerably safe, illustrates how powerfull those short snippets of Solidity are.

Upgradable contracts.

It is not convenient but not that hard to program contracts in a way so that they can be upgraded. One can argue that the mechanims to make them upgradable in effect keeps them centralized. That is, someone needs to have that backdoor key that allows for a complete change of the machinery after it is deployed.

That's true for the simplest cases, and not necessarily wrong for them. It's quite certain that a complete layer will spring up to deal with these questions, a *name service* similar to the very successful *domain name service* (DNS) that translates domain names in web site addresses to IP numbers. Everytime you type `wikileaks.org` into your browser, it is behind the scenes translated to an IP number like `195.35.109.44`. And if they have to change jurisdiction and move their servers, just this number is updated, the name stays the same. On the lowest level, the Internet works perfectly fine using just those numbers and that's how it started. But since long, the layer of names on top of the numbers is considered an integral part of the Internet. It will be the same with smart contracts, the important ones will not be addressed using their addresses like `0xBB9bc244D798123fDe783fCc1C72d3Bb8C189413`.

And that will be one point of indirection where updates to contract code become possible in a natural way.

But there exist ways today, by chaining contracts in an intelligent way and even a DAO can be made fixable by a majority decision by its investors.

All these mechanisms are by default attack vectors. A way to get in and change a contract from what it should be to something hijacked. But the importance of this aspect dictates that solutions and best practices have to be found.

Reversible transactions.

There will also be a layer on top of the irreversible layer to allow for reversible transactions. It is perfectly easy to program the reversal of a transaction today. You just send the Ether or whatever you got back. As part of the smart contract mechanism that you are setting up. Based on some sensible condition. Of course you might sometimes run into the problem that the funds are not there any more if you implement it in a naïve way. But whatever the mechanisms are that you deem appropriate to allow for a safe reversal – inevitably they will include timeouts and bonds – you can implement that on top of the basic layer we have today.

Even the basic layer is not based on irreversibility, at all. Because when a transaction runs out of gas, everything it did is reversed immediately. One can abort any contract call the same while it is still executing. Not from the outside when calling it, but by programming it that way.

However, from the point that a transaction is complete, the basic layer will remain with the irreversibility paradigm as anything else would have ripple effects that make state across the entire system unreliable. And this is quite special.

Test tools.

There are unique, new challenges when programming decentralized code. It is difficult to test anything that runs on a network. But programs in Ethereum behave differently than normal distributed code. It's not even trivial to test a snippet of Ethereum code offline and isolate them for testing them 'in a vacuum' as is usual. So both *sysem testing* and *unit testing* are difficult.

Tools are emerging that allow for easy testing of some of the new basics. It is rather clear what's needed and it will be rather straight forward to provide programmers what they need.

Reusing code.

Libraries for Ethereum will emerge that are well audited and tested. For basic functionalities, e.g. cryptography, third party, battle–tested libraries written in other languages, e.g. C, will become available with EVM 2.0.

Stabilizing the clients.

Finally, it would be good to get the clients stable, which are not written in Solidity or anything but are normal programs. Currently, major upgrades and updates continue to introduce new bugs and no EVM program is safe when it runs on clients that are not hardened. It's the equivalent of a flawless program in an exploding space shuttle.

Is Ethereum Legal?

Smart contracts may require a new contract law.

Smart contracts will work, no matter if they are buggy or not, whether their intent is legal, criminal or they are outlawed whole-sale. They are called contracts for a reason but the guarantee of execution they have built in is something our legal systems are not prepared for. That notion does simply not exist in current law and no one knows how judges and law makers will react.

The fact that smart contracts can't really be located, as they run in many different places at the same time, is not something provided for in our current legislations and regulations. In effect it now leads to the situation that a smart contract is subject to every jurisdiction where it is executed. It may be legal in some and illegal in some others all at the same time.

This is a problem for start ups as well as the core Ethereum entities. *COALA,* founded by Constance Choi and Primavera di Filippi, is an initiative that works to reduce the legal uncertainty about blockchains, produce accessible papers[135] on the matter and keep lawmakers from doings something rash.

---

135 COALA working groups – http://coala.global/projects/

Regulation could break blockchain technology.

It would come at a huge cost for progress in commerce, if existing regulation was applied straight as it is now, reducing blockchains to varying forms of currency.

Especially those functions could be outlawed, as side effect, that allow things that were previously impossible or impractical and therefore weren't considered when today's regulations were made. It could hit the very elements of automation that make smart contracts powerful and which could serve as foundation for new, fairer market mechanisms. Automatic execution of contracts itself could be declared to be against the law, because there is just no way to stop immoral or clearly criminal contracts, or to stop contracts violating the law in *some* country.

> As with cash, it will be impossible to stop all unlawful activities.

The quandaries here are obviously similar to those the Internet itself poses, and we might see national initiatives to address them akin to the the firewall around China.

Tax-evasion, money laundering, drugs, terrorism.

Banking is one of the most highly regulated industries and Bitcoin is certainly in the crosshairs of regulators around the globe. Cryptocurrencies got a different status in different parts of the world, and whether they are officially categorized as a currency, a value store or a good is relevant for how a transaction in a cryptocurrency is taxed. And therefore, how easily bitcoins, or Ether, can be used for tax-evasion.

But the bigger issues are money laundering, trade in illegal goods and terrorism. In the eyes of regulators, bitcoins have been shown to be a currency of choice for criminals, and its features are found to be ideal for shady deals by design. Maybe they also read some Cypherpunk prose talking of war until one side is completely defeated.

Now the piqued wrath of the regulators hangs above the blockchain world like Damocles' sword. Any exciting new project or start up could be hit as a test[136] or show of force with dire consequences for the creators. No one will know if the regulators just wait and watch until a target becomes sufficiently high profile to strike. This both stifles innovation, confirms the Cypherpunks' points and inspires innovations like Zcash.

And it's a reason why blockchain startup headquarters have gravitated to Switzerland and the UK and development to Berlin and Amsterdam. It's also why big corporations had a very hard time to get behind Ethereum or any blockchain, as they could not be seen to have too much interest in something so close to shady Bitcoin.

Ethereum is way more potent than Bitcoin when abused, for the creation of all sorts of illegal markets. With Ethereum, ordering, paying and delivery of digital goods

---

136 As opposed to European Continental Law, the Anglo-Saxon system is happy with courts to create new law when new circumstances so require. A usual procedure is for state agencies to sue companies to 'test' whether their interpretation of existing rules will hold in the court of law or result into new law being created in the form of the verdict against you. There is no way to be on the safe side before a judge ruled about it. As a founder this can land you in prison or, fearing that, you have incentive to settle for crushing sums and pay all your costs for the test yourself. Kind of a public service.

becomes fully integrated. All phases of a trade are covered, in part protected by strong encryption. The content is there in the Usenet[137] at any rate. But making a profit on it will become so much easier.

The way regulators tackle the problem today is by putting the onus on the interface between regular money and the blockchain currencies, i.e.: enforcing know-your-customer (KYC) and anti-money-laundering (AML) rules for every client of cryptocurrency exchanges. And this actually helped the Ethereum community to have a chance against the The DAO hackers: without the KYC of the exchanges, they could cash out a lot easier.

But this will become less and less efficient, the wider the range of products becomes that can be bought with cryptocurrencies: when one both receives and spends money using crypto, one doesn't need to go through the exchanges and can evade their KYC.

Regulation could target end users, developers or market players.

Targeting end users helped reducing illegal file sharing, but the game changer was making legal, commercial music downloading painless.

Targeting the developers will help little once the technology is online. Bitcoin does not need a whole lot of maintenance. Ethereum is basically made for being extended, by writing smart contracts on it, without any form of maintenance to its core system.

There are other fields where we don't allow everything that's possible, for ethical reasons. But not even banks want

---

137 An older and less popular part of the Internet for forums and sharing files, not directly reachable via browser and virtually uncensored.

the development to stop at this point, hoping for productivity gains to be had from blockchain technology rather than fearing its impact. And since at least spring 2016 there are so many big brands pushing for blockchain business it is hard to imagine they could all end up embarrassed.

There is a clear sentiment in the community that Bitcoin will not remain what it is today but may become ether useless or outlawed once perfect anonymity is added using zero knowledge proofs (see pg. 128), which is basically what Zcash is. People are watching that space now for sure.

On the other hand, the term blockchain is a household name in the industry at this point and cited with no further explanation in the Financial Times. All major banks and IT companies seem to be funding blockchain research. Companies of ever more industries feel they have to be seen doing something with blockchain.

This level of interest would indicate that established corporations might use their lobbying power to make sure that blockchains are not outlawed wholesale even if Zcash should be outlawed. A rather surprising development.

The collection if identifying data is a means to prevent action.

This is worth contemplating: we are used meanwhile to conflating security and loss of privacy. But this is only because privacy has to be given up, the way things work today, to allow to persecute and punish, *after* the fact. If we could fully reliably *prevent*, then the need to punish would fall by the wayside. And with it the need for identifying data: if the prevention itself worked without knowing identities then there is no need left to collect identities in the Orwellian way happening today.

That's not a new principle. Locks mostly don't report everyone who tries to open them but fails to provide the right key. They don't care about identity, they care about keys. There are locks tied to an alarm but also that mechanism is for prevention and not identity–based.

If one looks closer, the identity of a would be–perpetrator is never what actually matters to anyone. What matters is what the intended action is, to prevent it, and only after that fails, to know who to re–educate and confiscate from to make the victim whole. Only when the damage is done, does identity matter. If prevention can be complete, the argument for pro–actively infringing on privacy – our current default modus operandi for security – would be lost.

In the worst case this will result into some nightmarish Minority Report–like scenario where people are punished before they even do anything. But intent is punishable today. And the approach of prevention would *not* need punishment to work, that is the whole point.

It need not differentiate between honest and criminal mistakes to work. What remains is that it would curtail the ability to even try something forbidden, as choice, and then later argue in court why it was necessary, life saving, not even wrong in the first place or forbidden only by mistake. It would take away some gray zones where laws are on the books but not executed upon.

The blueprint for the prevention approach is how Bitcoin guarantees fairness, without the need for a third party. How it works completely without arbitration and legal overhead, because the core function simply can't go wrong in the first place. In that sense, it has its own regulation programmed right into its fabric. And that really is the essence of why it works.

On a higher level this could be augmented into a dedicated regulations layer.

Blockchains could mean a quantum leap in how regulation works: *ex-ante* instead of ex-post.

Blockchains could automate compliance and could allow us to move from writing rules in the legal sphere, which are per-se, just words, towards preventing things from going wrong in the first place, by coding rules as smart contracts that cannot be broken during execution. Rules that can be implemented by regulators themselves, or coded by businesses and audited by regulators as concrete interpretation of relevant regulation, *before* things are set in motion.

Pro–active regulation might require additional layers in the blockchain protocols on top of what we have now, but these will emerge at any rate. There are blockchains in development now, like Hyperledger or Corda, that have auditing nodes as part of their basic design.

If contracts that go against regulations simply don't execute – by using certificates to check permissions – then *a lot* of today's ex-post prosecution and fact-finding regulations would become obsolete. And if a certificate-based system could be established that effectively controls who can *do* what, without revealing *who* actually acts, all those privacy intrusions that states have been able to declare necessary over the last decades, would become a lot harder to justify.

All the personal information being collected and hoarded is there to identify and *find* you: in case you do something wrong. In case you are the wanted target for a product advertisement. Ex–ante regulation would eliminate any need to find you, to find out about you, to be allowed and commissioned to hoard data about you.

And we did not arrive at this liberating prospect by chance. This reversal was an explicit goal of the crypto community since the late 80's. It's what the Cypherpunks fight their war for, in the course of which they invented the 'weapons' cryptocurrency and blockchains as a means for exactly one thing: to preserve, and regain privacy.

CONTEXT

"The foundation is being laid for a dossier society, in which computers could be used to infer individuals' life-styles, habits, whereabouts, and associations from data collected in ordinary consumer transactions.

"Uncertainty about whether data will remain secure against abuse by those maintaining or tapping it can have a 'chilling effect,' causing people to alter their observable activities."

David Chaum, 1985

Cypherpunks!

"Cypherpunks write code."

Eric Hughes, 1993

Cypherpunks are a serious bunch. They are about fighting governments and corporations to save our civilization, and their weapon is code.

Blockchains and cryptocurrencies did not come about by chance.

They were sought after since the late 80's as essential, technological corner stones to preserve personal freedom in the face of governments and corporations that started equipping themselves with computers.

The decentralized timestamping feature of blockchains, for example, is not a newly discovered side effect of blockchains. It was, instead, the very goal that *hash–chaining* was invented for in the 90's: proving that a document existed at a certain time without needing a centralized service for that. Which was later used as a storage component in the creation of Bitcoin.

Behavioral changes under surveillance.

David Chaum wrote a paper in 1985 called

> *"Security without Identification:*
> *Transaction Systems to Make Big Brother Obsolete."*[138]

This work is one of the roots of the Cypherpunk movement. Its title reads exactly like what we find block-chains could make possible now: a way to regulate without sacrificing privacy. If at the risk of replacing Big Brother with Minority Report. Just kidding. But observe Chaum's pun with the publication date.

Chaum was concerned with the *chilling effect* of surveillance, channeling Huxley really who predicted in 1958 that after openly suppressive dictatorships we would be facing more subtle means of control next:

> *"it now looks as though the odds were more in favor of something like Brave New World than of something like 1984. ... government through terror works on the whole less well than government through the non-violent manipulation of the environment and of the thoughts and feelings of individual men, women and children."* [139]

Among other things, Chaum described *anonymous digital cash* in his paper and addressed the *double spending* problem.

Privacy in an open society.

At this point in time, we have gone down the road Chaum was warning about – just as a judgement of the

---

138 https://www.cs.ru.nl/~jhh/pub/secsem/chaum1985bigbrother.pdf
139 Huxley, *Brave New World Revisited*, 1958 –
https://www.huxley.net/bnw-revisited/

technology in use now – but in the late 1980's that didn't look so inevitable and a movement emerged, called Cypherpunks, who sought to use cryptography to fight surveillance and targeting.

One of their founders, Eric Hughes, wrote in "*A Cypherpunk's Manifesto*"[140] in 1993:

> "*Privacy is necessary for an open society in the electronic age. ... We cannot expect governments, corporations, or other large, faceless organizations to grant us privacy ... We must defend our own privacy if we expect to have any.*"

Hughes was part of a group that started gathering in 1992 on whom the term 'Cypherpunks' was originally coined, in jest, and who started an anonymous mailing list,[141] whose members where discussing all things related to cryptography, soon read by hundreds of people who were then all called Cypherpunks.

It is said that there was rarely *consensus* on that list about anything and that some views presented were extreme. But there were senior people from hi-tech companies, and well-known researchers taking part.

And they wrote code.

The Crypto Wars.

Cryptography had long been a science that was practiced in secrecy by the military and governments. This changed when the US government published the *Data Encryption Standard* (DES) in 1975, because financial institu-

---

140 A Cypherpunk Manifesto, 1993 – https://w2.eff.org/Privacy/
    Crypto/Crypto_misc/cypherpunk.manifesto
141 Cypherpunks mailing list archive   https://github.com/Famicoman/
    cypherpunks-mailing-list-archives/tree/master/cryptome.org

tions needed strong cryptography to secure wired money transfers.

But cryptography was still classified as munitions and with that, export controlled. This was an effort to make sure the know–how would not end up in the Eastern Bloc and US IT corporations had to make case-by-case export license request when cryptography was part of a product.

At home, the agencies successfully pushed for keeping commercial encryption weak, so they could brute force any communication open with the help of their super computers.

Hughes was careful to lay out in his Manifesto that the Cypherpunks did not seek secrecy, but privacy and made clear what the difference was. And that crypto was needed for both.

"Privacy is not secrecy. A private matter is something one doesn't want the whole world to know, but a secret matter is something one doesn't want anybody to know. Privacy is the power to selectively reveal oneself to the world."

Cypherpunks encouraged civil disobedience and enganged in activism. T–shirts were made with forbidden crypto source code printed on them, programs printed as books to be able to legally export them. But most of all, Open Source programs were written that allowed for the free, private application of crypto, for example to encrypt emails.

And there was probably no little disappointment when people just didn't pick up on it. When it became possible to, without cost and no extra effort, encrypt every single email, but people just didn't and instead flocked to centralized services. Or web sites continued to serve unencrypted pages by default although every page could, at little extra effort, be served as well secured as a credit card transaction.

Creating background noise.

The idea was, and is, that of creating background noise to help obfuscating what might be vulnerable. The game theory behind it is a little bit like voting. Not everything needs to be encrypted, and your own efforts technically don't make a difference. You are not really protecting anything. But when practiced by everyone, total surveillance becomes a lot harder. And it might prevent for you to end up on a list you don't want to be on for matching some pattern.

> *"For privacy to be widespread it must be part of a social contract. People must come and together deploy these systems for the common good. Privacy only extends so far as the cooperation of one's fellows in society."*

That only weak keys were allowed – which put the entire digital US economy at risk to be hacked by criminals or antagonistic state players – made the argument for creating noise just the more compelling.

Even if encryption was weak, if everything was encrypted, this would still make it very hard for governments – and corporations – to find the patterns they would be looking for. Even if they could break any individual key, they would constantly have to decide which one to spend the resources on. And would thus be effectively hindered to establishing patterns and applying dragnet techniques.

The end of privacy.

The war ended in 2000, when the US export restrictions on crypto were dropped. There is know–how available now, and privacy tools, thanks to the Cypherpunks, even if the war for informational self–determination was lost.

Chaum's 1985 proposal on how to change the default flow of information has, by and large, not been picked up because economic and national security incentives stood against it.

Instead, we have the first generation of people now who were incentivized to give up as much information about their formative years as possible. That's a daring, large scale social experiment. And as a result now everyone knows someone who has lost a job because of facebook.

Turning the tables.

Meanwhile, it all escalated to a more total war where secret services get more and more legal rights so they can better protect us and WikiLeaks now indiscriminately publishes everything they can get, denying the logic that some functions of governments, parties, corporations, political activism or whistle blowing might legitly benefit from and deserve secrecy.

Clinton lost Michigan by some 12,000 votes, Wisconsin by 27,000, Pennsylvania by 68,000. Podesta emails anyone? So it came from a Russian server? She was certainly in the crosshairs of one aggrieved posse. The Cypherpunks might, just might, be changing the course of history by selective targeting and timing. And their aim is certainly 'the establishment.'

But it needed a charismatic, hipster[142] whistle blower – Snowden, qua definition *not really* a Cypherpunker – to convince the public that the Bourne movie scripts were in fact based on NSA insider knowledge.

Finally, reality looks like the action we deserved all along, complete with close–drawn curtains in secret hotel rooms and presidential planes forced to land. Everyone knows Snowden would be rotting in jail but for the albino chief punk sending his girl friend to rescue him to Moscow – now that's a story people can relate to, including love and death,[143] acted out in full public view. And sales went up for the original Cypherpunk message.

Web services switched to the secure protocol that had been available for years. Even Apple now sees the economic value in being more open about how they were guardians of your privacy all along.

Then after 11/9, demand for privacy–respecting messaging tools like Signal[144] quadrupled within a week.[145]

Anonymous transactions.

The Cypherpunks defined the ability to make *anonymous transactions* – like using cash – as key to being able to have any privacy. They ranked it up there with being able to encrypt communication.

---

142 He hides behind not heaving a beard, obviously.

143 Solidary confinement works as surrogate for death in story–telling.

144 Signal is WhatsApp with privacy – https://whispersystems.org/

145 Signal downloads up 400% since Trump's election – http://www.marketplace.org/2016/11/15/world/encryption-app-signal-sees-400-growth-election.

Otherwise *behaviour patterns* would still give away everything about you – what we now call *meta data* and what the agencies claim is the harmless part of the data.

Accordingly, the attempts to create a cryptocurrency were not a random strand of Cypherpunk activity, but elemental to their cause, from the start. And in a way, what they had actually been looking for has arrived only now, in the form of Zcash.

It was also clear that it doesn't end with anonymous payment but ideally encompass an entire *digital business flow* – the step from Bitcoin to Ethereum.

Our digital doppelgangers.

Meanwhile, in the real world, we have gotten used to unknowable sets of information about us being used in real time to decide whether we should get a job, a lease, a loan, an upgrade or a spouse. Anyone would be hard pressed to make a good guess how many places the world over information about them might be stored. How many times do we hear as excuse that someone does what he does because the computer says so.

The mechanisms are not necessarily secret and rarely illegal. We consent as we see the business case. Many feel it really, really just doesn't matter at all. It just happens to be the opposite of *informational self–determinism*.

And while the US debate is about how much the agencies should be allowed to spy at home, the rest of the world has resigned to the unescapable, unfettered, recourse-less, invisible reach of NSA, GCHQ & Co.

Sure, Topaz might have averted WWIII. But people are being routinely killed now because they match certain *patterns*. And while terrorists have successfully been hunted this way since the 70's, the difference is that there was something like due process at some time. The 'targets' don't have to be officially at war now, they don't even have to be non-US citizens anymore.

If matching a pattern is good for life and death decisions at this point, how to complain about its 'lesser' applications, aimed at making our lives safer and more comfortable.

But since more and more services are extended to us, or not, because we fit a pattern, the bubble of confirmation bias we all have around us at any rate is enforced by algorithms selling us the world they can predict we'll find preferrable.

We all know that's how scoring and ad targeting work.

But the political others – all those who obviously have gone mad and don't make any sense when they speak – could not see what you see anymore now, even if they *wanted*. The membranes of our bubbles are not strictly under our control any more. Mulled Huxely 60 years ago:

> *"The victim of mind-manipulation does not know that he is a victim. To him, the walls of his prison are invisible, and he believes himself to be free. That he is not free is apparent only to other people."*

You know how you look to the other side.

That's what the Cypherpunks are on about.

That's where blockchains are coming from.

The Road to Bitcoin

Switching back to the tech, looking at how it all came together is a great opportunity to recap the building blocks of blockchains.

The decentralized mailing list.

Establishing anonymous communication was an obvious starting point for the Cypherpunks. In 1992 Hughes set up that anonymous email remailer, the Cypherpunk mailing list. It would basically accept emails, strip away the sender info and forward them to the intended receiver. Totally trackable by the *Five Eyes* today but back then, it might have helped.

After a falling out about moderation – or, censorship – of those emails, the Cypherpunks Distributed Remailer (CDR) was set up in 1997, a network of independent mailing list nodes. If one CDR node crashed or its oper-ator started censoring emails, the list would continue to work and relay all emails coming in. Unless everyone decided to censor the same email.

No matter what CDR node you sent a message to, all other CDR nodes would receive it, too, and relay it to all listening to that node.

Pretty much how blockchain clients work today.

Hashes as cyber valuables.

Like all other email infrastructure, the Cypherpunk mailing list would soon have to battle with spam. A problem that Google et al. Later solved by total recentralization of email.

But the main thinking during the day was that emails should simply not be quite that cost–free for the sender, to incur a cost on spammers. One idea was to require some form of micropayment for each email sent. Another was to require a *proof of work*: show that you had busied your CPU for a short moment, for every email you want to send. Which would suffice to slow spammers down and put them out of business.

The idea that *proof of computational effort* could be seen as *digital value* goes back to anti–spam research Cynthia Dwork and Moni Naor did at IBM in 1992.[146] In 1997 Cypherpunk *Adam Back* – today shaping Bitcoin's future with *Blockstream*,[147] – proposed *Hashcash*[148] as an implementation of this principle.

An email would be hashed again and again, with a different random nonce added each go, until the resulting hash, by chance, showed a required number of leading zeros.

---

146 http://www.wisdom.weizmann.ac.il/~naor/PAPERS/pvp.pdf

147 Blockstreams – https://blockstream.com

148 Hashcash proof–of–work – http://hashcash.org

This nonce was added to the email's meta information when sending the email. On the receiver's side, one quick calculation sufficed to check that the nonce was valid. And with that have mathematical prove – rather than having to trust – that some puzzle work had been performed.

It's exactly what blockchains do – or more precisely what drives the proof–of–work consensus algorithm. And Bitcoin and Ethereum use the original Hashcash algorithm for it.

There are two ways to look at it: for one, the proof of work creates scarcity and with this, value. Because that was the idea: emails should cost something.

On the other hand this is just about slowing things down. But reliably, provably so.

And that *is* at the heart of proof–of–work: miners can't be allowed to propose blocks as fast as they can. Being just a little erlier than everyone else would be worth a lot of money. This would immediately clogg the blockchain network. Proof–of–work is the fair way to slow things down and give it a rhythm.

The important part is: it's non–interactive. It does not require more communication to reduce communication.

Cryptocurrency as means of anonymous transactions.

Besides communication, Cypherpunks always had a private microcurrency high on their wish list. Wrote Hughes in his Manifesto:

>   *„We the Cypherpunks are dedicated to building anonymous systems. We are defending our privacy with cryptography, with anonymous mail forwarding systems, with digital signatures, and with electronic money."*

Cryptocurrency among the top four bullet points.

And not for money from nothing, or digital convenience. But for its role to enable privacy.

There is the opinion that an outsider had to come along to relax the desired spec a bit, settle for *pseudonymity* instead of *anonymity* and get it done as good as possible.

b–money proposes copying everything.

In 1998, the concept of *b-money*,[149] was described by *Wei Dai*[150] on the Cypherpunk mailing list.

Inversing the logic that emails should cost something to send, and how Hashcash was a solution to this, Dai proposed to anchor the value of a digital currency in the scarcity of the nonces. The *work* could be seen as the act of *minting a currency*. The nonces themselves would be the valuables. The question was how to settle ownership.

Dai proposed that *every participant should hold a copy of everyone's accounts*. b-money would be transferred by broadcasting the transactions to everybody else. If there was disagreement, *every participant would go over correcting the affected accounts themselves*, manually.

There was no algorithmic consensus. Apart from that though, this sounds very much like Bitcoin.

---

149 b–money – http://www.weidai.com/bmoney.txt

150 A pseudonym, by the way, that can only be read as a entropian pun, "why die?"

bit gold is chaining hashes.

Nick Szabo added the next idea with his *bit gold*[151] proposal: *chaining hashes* to create an ever longer chain of *"unforgeably costly bits."*

The idea for a block chain is dating back to a series of papers by *Haber* and *Stornetta*, starting 1991. They were thinking about reliably timestamping documents and came up with a (central) service that would nest the hash of its last timestamped document into the next one.

Then everyone holding a document from that service could attest to the validity of the document timestamped immediately before, and after, without the help of that service. That would give everyone three options to find whitness to the correctness of their timestamp, making somewhat independent of that central service. Haber and Stornetta also came up with *blocks* that bundled documents together.

With bit gold, the question remained how to keep people honest and not just copy the precious bits when transferring them to someone else. In Szabo's scheme, a registry would keep track of who the string of precious bits was assigned to *last*. One could *sign their bits over to someone else* by adding a new nonce and hash that incorporated the previous top chain hash and the ownership transfer of the previous owner. The registry would identify *ownership by a public key* and whoever had the corresponding private key to it would be able to control it: i.e. sign it over to somebody else. So spending it was the act of signing a signed hash chain head over to someone else.

---

151 It's not quite clear when he might have first thought or written about it but it is part of the canonical narrative.

Smart contracts.

Allegedely in 1994[152] Nick Szabo also described the idea for smart contracts. The idea was less about unstoppable cryptocurrency–based agreements but for a better form of law.

Cypherpunks were well aware that hopping through different jurisdictions made it quite hard for law enforcement to chase cyber vigilants. It just took desperately much time for law enforcement to get at the servers by legal means to inspect the intruders' traces.

How smart contracts are today executed in many different jurisdictions at the same time is not quite the same but it helps making them unstoppable in a similar way. It would take forever to, by legal means, force all owners of all nodes in all jurisdictions to stop a particular contract from executing. If a selective off–switch, per contract, was implemented in the first place.

The missing part.

The only thing that had not been found by 1997 was how to properly decentralize that registry of accounts.

Szabo proposed a traditional Byzantine Fault Tolerant server network for the task, i.e. using a technology that many in the blockchain space now want to go back to.

But Szabo, Dai and Back had brought all the elements to the table – most of all: nonces, hash–chaining and independent arbitration – that would form the core of blockchains' proof–of–work consensus algorithm, the open-ended, signature-less, game-incentivized consensus with probabilistic finality.

---

152 *ditto.*

The dot com bubble happened, a lot of centralized, digital currencies emerged, were bought up by the banks and died the death of the electric car. David Chaum's own start up, *DigiCash* might just have been too early but also rested on a client–server architecture.

"I hope it's obvious it was only the centralized nature of those systems that doomed them", some Satoshi Nakamoto later had to say about them.

But for a decade, silence.

What is Bitcoin?

"What is needed is an electronic payment system based on cryptographic proof instead of trust."

Bitcoin white paper, 2008

Bitcoin is the first *decentralized* digital currency.

The payment system was purportedly invented by some 'Satoshi Nakamoto', of whom no one knows who he is. Several people have claimed to be Nakamoto but no claim was convincing.

The idea for Bitcoin was floated on a cryptography mailing list in 2008 and a first client released as Open Source in 2009. The Bitcoin white paper[153] is still required reading for any blockchain programmer and lays out the basic principles beautifully. Nakamoto stated that he wrote the paper kind–of backwards, clearing his thoughts first by coding the actual client.

---

153 Bitcoin whitepaper – https://bitcoin.org/bitcoin.pdf

As we saw, the individual inventions it uses were not original but dating back up to twenty years. Still the system on the whole kicked off a revolution.

The whitepaper does not talk about changing the world but is concerned with enabling micro transactions by reducing costs and alleviating the need for trust, to end the situation that

> *"Merchants must be wary of their customers, hassling them for more information than they would otherwise need."[154]*

Bitcoin is b—money. And bit gold. And Hashcash.

Bitcoin merged b-money's approach to have *everyone hold a copy of everything*, particularly of the registry of who owns what, and *ownership expressed using public keys for account numbers* — but now in the form of an entire chained history of both minting (mining) and transactions: one single chain of bit gold instead of a collection of private ones. The decentralization of the registry was folded into the minting process.

One indirection was added between the 'work' and the value – the nonce itself is *not* used as the value now – and the idea of timestamping through some trusted outside mechanism was retired for what was actually only needed: unambiguity about the *order* of transactions. Which is slightly easier to solve.

Something else had been missing in previous proposals: the adjustment of the system over time to the fact that computers get more powerful. Bitcoin has a dynamic

---

154 *ibid.*

adjustment to that built in, which makes something else available in the system as by–product: a measure of the collective computational power that had gone into creating the chain of blocks.

And this parameter allowed for something essential: non–interactive consensus.

Because it could be used as *objective* anchor of consensus between nodes: confronted with different versions of a chain – i.e. with different last blocks – a node should have all incentive to elect that chain as 'truth' that has the most computational effort invested into it.

And this was how Wei Dai's proposal arbitration on the personal level was enahnced with an objective yardstick, so 'disagreement' on the world state could always be solved by looking at what truth had more work invested into it.

That's where Adam Back says: *"Bitcoin is just HashCash extended with inflation control."* And Nick Szabo: *"Bitcoin is bit gold."* Just Wei Dai stated how he was surprised one could make money mining Bitcoin.

Nakamoto at first seemed to not know about bit gold, but later advised:

> *"Bitcoin is an implementation of Wei Dai's b-money*
> *… and Nick Szabo's Bitgold proposal."*[155]

Bitcoin was made to dis–intermediate banks.

The whitepaper introduces Bitcoin as *"a solution to the double-spending problem using a peer-to-peer network"* and in its

---

155 https://bitcointalk.org/index.php?topic=342.msg4508#msg4508

first sentence describes the goal to send money *"without going through a financial institution."*

And this is in fact how it works. Transactions take place between users directly but all users of Bitcoin can verify any transaction and they are stored on all of the 7,000 Bitcoin nodes that are online at any given time so they can never be reversed.

Bitcoin may have 10,000,000 users.

No one knows how many Bitcoin nodes exist in total as there is no central mechanism to count them and many nodes just come online and sync when their user wants to use Bitcoin, and go offline again after that. The number of nodes also has nothing to do with the number of Bitcoin users, because you can use Bitcoin by using web pages alone. The number of online wallets will have reached 10,000,000 in December 2016.

But of course to mine, you want to be online all the time.

Bitcoins got worth real money.

That bitcoins ever got worth significant amounts of money sure looks like a modern miracle.

After all, it is not only not backed by gold, but by nothing. There is no lower bound price support. Its value is purely a matter of supply and demand. But at some point, exchanges popped up where people started trading bitcoins and a price in USD emerged.

Bitcoin prices went up very slowly. Some people who had bought bitcoins for a few cents a-piece were very proud when they sold at $2. Until a frenzy in 2013 saw an all-time high of $1124.76 on 29 November 2013, up from just US$13.36 on 5 January at the start of the year.

It then came back down just as fast, plateaued some time at $900 then $700 all in all sinking ineroxably until languishing around $200 all summer 2015. Since then it is going up again at almost the same slow speed, at the end of 2016 hovering around $700 again.

Bitcoin matured in shady niches.

The use of Bitcoin for criminal activity has attracted the angry attention of financial regulators.

And by convincingly many parameters, Silkroad was in fact the killer app for Bitcoin. Using it for buying stuff from the darknet will have been a main pillar for its usefulness during its first years.

This was not the argument of the Cypherpunks though. They argued that one should have privacy in one's business. Not that one should have freedom to engage in illegal dealings. And that you could have the one without the other was Chaum's central point.

But anyway, with drugs becoming legalized in more and more jurisdictions, Bitcoin's story echoes how photography and film went through early years during which interest was kept alive and progress financed by returns from pornography, until the technology had matured to a degree that it could be used for more reputable things.

There were allegations of assassination contracts in the Silkroad trial, but those were likely launched to sway jurors to agree to a life sentence for the operator, and not substantiated. Assassinations are depressingly cheap in real life and don't need complex payment technology to be a market. However, the *assassination contract* has become for blockchains what child pornography is for the Internet: the killer argument for regulation even before financing of asymmetric warfare comes into the picture.

All this made corporations weary to even consider taking Bitcoin seriously. And very happy when the term 'blockchain' came around and gave them a chance to talk about the core invention without having to pronounce 'Bitcoin'. Now there are edit wars going on at Wikipedia where Bitcoin is being deleted from the definition for blockchains.

Bitcoin was not made to scale.

Bitcoin is now being called a toy, or an experiment, because many people have given up on the hopes to ever see it scale. They are counting Back out too fast.

And that it was not designed to scale does not necessarily mean it is a failure now. It does work for its purpose and a lot of people are using it. It was just not invented for industry scale, or world-wide payment processing.

Bitcoin saves businesses money now.

Early 2015, the number of merchants accepting bitcoins for products and services passed 100,000, among them big names like Dell or Expedia.

Instead of 2–3% typically imposed by credit card processors, merchants pay no direct fees, and customers pay around $0.05 − 0.10 when paying with Bitcoin.

Bitcoin loses people money.

Digital theft – from *centralized* Bitcoin services, the irony – has exacted a heavy price on Bitcoin fans.

The most successful early exchange that traded bitcoins vs USD, *MtGox*, was originally an online trading card platform, hacked in PHP and utterly unprepared to deal with the amounts of real money soon sloshing through it. It lost its users half a million bitcoins over the years, a value of $300 million when it finally went down in a big scandal in early 2014.

Somewhat surprisingly, really, it was not the last such event and the Bitcoin community proved utterly resilient against the lesson that re-centralizing the task of holding bitcoins to cloud services not only a somewhat antithetical but also dangerous choice. For a tender created to work in a decentralized fashion.

In late 2016 the latest such event was the loss of $60 million by Bitfinex.

Bitcoin might be a Silicon Valley unicorn bet.

Silicon Valley saw many investors betting big on Bitcoin. Rumor has it that they invested private money buying bitcoins. Then helped found Bitcoin-related companies, collected funding for them and invested the raised money into bitcoins, too. This would have pushed the Bitcoin price nicely while it gave the world a thousand and one flavors of bitcoin wallets.

Because ideas for what to actually do with all those start ups did not come easy. What was funded in 2014 sure was hilarious.

Silicon Valley was less interested to hear about other cryptocurrencies and staunchly defended Bitcoin against new comers.

So the the blockchain space shifted East.

Bitcoin has a bad centralization problem.

Today's blockchains need miners and because Bitcoin mining uses crazy amounts of electricity, Bitcoin mining is now concentrated in China were people found ways to use entire hydro power plants for mining bitcoins.

That's not how it was meant to be. Bitcoin mining was supposed to happen on the computers of those using Bitcoin and for the first years that is in fact what happened.

But ASICs came along and mining became a hot business when the bitcoin price shot up.

The big miners can change the course of history for Bitcoin if they decided to collude, in a similar way that they are now crucial for the survival of Ethereum Classic (see pg. 293).

Changing history is very much want you don't want to happen for a cryptocurrency.

The Ethereum Story

Ethereum is Vitalik Buterin's idea.

Traveling the Bitcoin world, physically, he wondered if there could be a better way than having to stop and amend the code of all blockchain clients whenever one wanted to add a new capability.

With a blockchain, starting and stopping it, kind-of defeats its purpose. You want a blockchain to be under no single authority and run forever, uninterrupted. The harder it would be to even convince people of making code changes to their clients in concert, the better, more protected the system.

Now, already with Bitcoin, transactions were essentially tiny scripts, if with clipped wings, restricted to three standard forms back then, for safety. The idea was to beef up the power of the virtual machine that executes these transactions – Bitcoin's VM – and make transactions be full fledged programs.

As mentioned, Vitalik likes to stress that the main change was *adding statefulness* to scripts, which follows quite naturally once transactions are considered *objects*[156] in the interplay of calculations that determine how one world state progresses to the next. And objects call each other.[157]

In the process, transaction code was also made Turing-complete, simply by adding the ability to have loops. Which was no big deal technically but required to address the problem of infinite loops.

The idea did not come to Vitalik in a vacuum and Yanislav Malahov assumed the title 'Godfather of Ethereum,' claiming he gave Vitalik the idea[158] when working with him to build a color coin wallet.

In 2013, after making himself a name as prodigy author at the Bitcoin Magazine, Vitalik was shopping around for jobs at Bitcoin startups. He was checking out Mastercoin and working on a color coin wallet with Yanislav for Ascribe, the company that since created BigChainDB, and based on it, IPDB, in pursuit of their vision of registering real–world art using a blockchain.

The way that color coins piggyback information onto a blockchain, for which the information is irrelevant and opaque, was the most powerful way to (ab-)use a blockchain back then if one wanted to – *without changing it* – create new functionality on top of it. And there was basically only one blockchain out there, Bitcoin.

Color coins had some shortcomings, which could be overcome, if the 'color' could be a made meaningful for the blockchain proper somehow, rather than being opaque

---

156 Object as in Object Oriented Programming, the mainstream design paradigm for program languages.

157 Actually objects were once supposed to send messages to each other, and to scale, blockchains might have to revisit that difference.

158 https://medium.com/@yanislav/king-of-bitcoin-god-father-of-ethereum-a9af9ecf56d5

for it, but without loosing the freedom to *change* its actual meaning and effect. That could be a description of Ethereum.

Vitalik published the Ethereum White Paper.

The core Ethereum people were basically all those who answered Vitalik's first email announcing the white paper[159] at the end of 2013. Many people then added their ideas and it went from there. Gavin Wood, a computer science Ph.D., wrote the more specific Yellow Paper[160] early 2014 that served as unifying blueprint for the multiple efforts at implementing the system.

Joe Lubin, a former hedge fund programmer, footed the bills to get a company structure off the ground, designed to secure the independence of Ethereum and as a legal path to the planned crowd-funding and pre-sale. Mid 2014 Vitalik was awarded a Peter Thiel Fellowship worth $100,000.

The white paper went through many iterations, the original version does not even exist anymore. But more than people tend to appreciate, the vision set forth there remained the overall guidance for everyone involved.

The Yellow Paper made sure that the *programming* itself did not influence important features ad-hoc. Where Bitcoin basically grew out of a concrete implementation, which became the de-facto spec, which all other implementation then had to copy (including its bugs :-) – Ethereum instead has an abstract specification in the Yellow Paper that eight implementations have been built from over time (listed with links pg. 332).

---

159 White paper   https://github.com/ethereum/wiki/wiki/White-Paper
160 Yellow Paper – http://gavwood.com/Paper.pdf

And then there was Ether.

Ethereum collected $18M USD in crowd-funding.

The pre-sale of Ether was at its time the second most successful crowdfunding drive ever. Ether were sold by the Ethereum Foundation for bitcoins and the equivalent of $18M USD was collected.

Unfortunately, the bitcoin price imploded within weeks and halved the means available for development. In fairness, they could not have sold all the bitcoins without crashing the market themselves. But a hedge might have been available to the re-inventors of finance.

Development was scattered across four languages, teams and cities.

Unimpressed by the losses, headquarters were created in Zug in Switzerland, Berlin and London.

A C++ team was hired in Berlin by Gavin Wood, the Go team was established by Jeffrey Wilcke in Amsterdam, PR was driven from London and the core people kept meeting, living and jousting with government officials in Zug, where the Ethereum Foundation has its seat.

Heiko Hees of Brainbot, a programming shop based in Mainz, Germany, rewrote the Python client that Vitalik had created as proof of concept and which remains the fertile testing ground for new ideas.

Martin Becze implemented the Javascript VM that is crucial for many tools in the ecosystem as it works in the browser, needs no installation and is super portable. He did that all on his own in a trailer in Indiana and showed up to the rest of the group only after he was done. The eggs were counted at that point and true to smart contract logic this meant he could not participate in the lush pre-mine and salary riches the other founders were meanwhile doling out to themselves.

Having independent implementations of the system was deemed to help robustness, as the clients would be used to test each other and one bug in one client can not bring the entire network down. The validity of this thinking was highlighted first during the beta phase in 2015 when the Go clients got stuck and the C++, Javascript and Python clients – and also the non-canonical Haskell and Java ones – kept working and sustained the network until the Go bug was fixed. The same happened a year later when attackers first knocked out the Go clients and then later the Rust clients. The network stayed up.

But it also creates an attack vector for splitting the network and it looks somewhat like everyone just went ahead using the language they liked most instead of bundling forces. Which is totally fair in Open Source.

And they delivered. Not only the product.

Joe Lubin founded Consensys in New York early 2015 and started providing a playground for every programmer who wanted a credible shot at a product made with Ethereum, seeding and supporting the dev community with salaries, news and tools from early on. Consensys was a programmer paradise with little pressure or directives from above before revenue-focus got a little more pronounced in 2016.

Silicon Valley, binging on Bitcoin, was notably absent. Only few Ethereum start ups, like String Labs are operating from there. The Ethereum Development office in Berlin certainly helped making the city 'a blockchain center of gravity,' as Gavin calls it.

For most of 2015 things developed as planned, if a little slower than hoped and on a tighter budget than it first looked. There were nagging worries that Ether pre-sale buyers might sue in case the system couldn't be shipped in time, or be too buggy. The voices in the forums, asking about how things fared, were indeed not only of understanding enthusiasts.

Coming into the Berlin office had a very special feel. It was the developer's dream, no investor pressure, no corporate BS. Just coders coding and in the most disciplined way. Well, many of them.

The self appointed dead lines were missed, predictably. The feature list was stripped down, wisely. By the end of 2015 the atmosphere got tense, the fun was over.

Then, the Ethereum guys proved all naysayers wrong and delivered, within the usual scope of delays, fits and improvisations, found with any software project.

The Amsterdam guys that is. As a consequence of the Foundation's decision to feature the Go client first. The correct calculation being that Go should be easier to get stable than C++.

The Frontier release in summer 2015 was deliberately low key, maybe to stay blurry enough about whether that was the launch or not. It really was, and it really was still all in pre-beta.

But the non-event that it was, media-wise, lead many watchers to conclude that Ethereum had not actually delivered. The traffic on the mainnet stayed very low. Sensing the opportunity, this lead to a spike in announcements from other blockchain projects.

The PR guy left and soon found a way to create real headlines. With The DAO (pg. 286).

The Ethereum Foundation, Consensys and EthCore finance development.

Today, the Ethereum Foundation, controlled as throughout by Vitalik, fully sponsors the Go and C++ clients and supports the Python and Javascript clients. Vitalik's research is expected to bring proof–of–stake consensus to Ethereum and give it better scale. The Foundation also supports the development of a new VM.

Brainbot shoulders most of the cost of the ongoing development of the Python client, the Hydrachain flavor and Raiden extension.

Joe Lubin's Consensys, the New York–based Ethereum hub, supports the non-canonical Haskell, and at one point the Java client. Joe keeps building out the ecosystem and when I asked him in spring 2016 if he was pumping Ether, he laughed and remarked that he always did all he could to make Ethereum a success. Absolutely.

Meanwhile, EthCore, mostly made up of former C++ guys and based in Berlin, have started over and offer their Rust[161] client now, Parity.

Separately, privateer Chris Holborne, concerned about the power of miners, keeps sponsoring independent research. He supported Vlad Zamfir for a long stretch,

---

161 Rust is a new, up and coming program language, more nimble than Go but safer than C++.

who now pays research on *Casper*, a proof-of-stake approach, partly out of his own pocket, partly from grants by the Ethereum Foundation and others.

Martin, let go by the Foundation at the end of 2015 when money got tight, just kept working anyway and realizes his pioneering design for the next Ethereum Virtual Machine that the entire ecosystem is waiting for, living off the land. Metaphorically.

There is hope for healthy competition.

This proliferation of clients, languages, teams and interests happened in Bitcoin, too. There is hope for a healthy competition through this. Almost everyone is on speaking terms with everyone else.

All protagonists know each other pretty well, so it doesn't necessarily hurt that there is no established mechanism of co-operation or to agree on protocol improvements, beyond a common forum and format in which to make proposals.[162]

There is some frustration. And while Consensys, Eth-Core and Brainbot are committed to commercialization, the Foundation and its men and women have more of a public goods perspective.

There are four somewhat different approaches for scalability in the works. The Parity and geth team started out focussing on different factors first — *state tree pruning*[163]

162 Ethereum Improvement Proposal (EIP) –
https://github.com/ethereum/EIPs

163 The state tree is the global Ethereum data. State tree pruning is a garbage collection of the storage on an individual machine. Technically one should never throw any old state away to be able to verify old blocks, re-doing all the way from the genesis block if necessary. Practically a lot of data points in the state tree cannot be

and *light client*[164] respectively. They have their own designs for the next steps without caring much about whether the other teams will pick their approach up, or when.

As for a new consensus model, more suitable to scaling, there is Vitalik's pragmatic approach: he is currently coding trials of his own version of Casper. Vlad is still more focussed on getting formal verification right with the help of *Greg Meredith*. Given that consensus is a hard problem that people have spent decades researching, this seems like a smart approach to avoid future catastrophic events. On the other hand the Cypherpunk ethos is, to make code.

Gavin is taking his own stab at sharding for the Parity client. Dominic Williams presents a different proposal for Dfinity that is based on *puzzle towers* to keep miners honest.

None of these efforts could be adopted by the existing Ethereum mainnet without a hard-fork. And as The DAO hard-fork showed, it is by no means guaranteed that everyone is going to be on board for the big change to go away from proof-of-work. As it would make very expensive mining hardware useless, one could assume that miners will lobby hard against it. But they might also just migrate to Zcash where the same hardware can be used.

---

reached anymore by future blocks and thus can be thrown away to make space. This massively reduces Parity's memory foot.

164 See pg. 102

What is The DAO?

As a matter of clever marketing, *Stephan Tual*, the former CMO of the Ethereum Foundation, named one DAO his company created 'The DAO'. It is not the only DAO, nor the only of its kind but it sure got all the press.

It became an epic enterprise, if not entirely as envisioned by its makers. For a time it looked so smart, sucking in $150,000,000 worth of Ether – before it was hacked and gave the Ethereum community a chance to show character.

The DAO *was* a great idea. Christoph Jentzsch, the actual founder of Slock.It, programmed the smart contracts for The DAO, which would collect money in form of Ether and act as incubator for Ethereum-related start up ideas.

Investors would vote for the ideas brought before The DAO with votes weighed by the size of their investment into the DAO. And a completely automated investing, voting and payout process. Once the money was paid in, no-one but the algorithms of the DAO controlled.

To be safe on the legal side, Christoph did not even deploy his code to the blockchain himself. He just posted the source and waited for curious people to try it out, then

Slock.It picked one that was funded with freshly mined Ether. To be extra safe.

Note that it made no difference to them who deployed The DAO as it was not to be controlled by anyone at any rate. But as the *A* in the name says, to be autonomous. Impartially reacting to any input.

To this day there are many contract instances of The DAO deployed on the mainnet, but only the one Slock.It chose to focus their PR on became the actual The DAO, by network effect.

Of course they hoped to finance Slock.It this way. And going in, they felt that maybe if $500,000 materialized through this strategy, they should consider themselves really lucky.

Instead, 15% of all Ether in existence poured in. After all, lots of Ether are held for speculation and The DAO promised to put the stale funds to work.

Core tech investment drought.

The original purpose of The DAO was sorely needed.

Despite the fact that $1.2 billion have been invested in blockchain start ups to date, there is a financing bottleneck for the core tech. Gavin feels that he would need $5 - $10 million to create a scalable version of Ethereum. Vlad finances Ethereum research for that from his own money.

The DAO would have solved this in a genius way — should those core projects have been able to make a convincing case to The DAO's investors. It would have been a fascinating evolution of blockchain crowdfunding to the next level, beyond pre–selling crypto tokens.

The unstoppable heist in broad daylight.

Now a heist in the blockchain world today necessarily happens in plain sight. Someone makes money flow in directions it should not, everyone sees it, no one knows who is behind it and no one can stop it.

So it came that one day in a technical chat, out of the blue, someone typed *"hey, I think The DAO is being hacked"* and really, funds where being transferred out of it at a steady rate, with – you knew it – no one able to stop it.

It went on for hours and proved nicely how smart contracts can in fact not be stopped. At least there is no button and no general backdoor if it is designed that way.

This was before The DAO had funded anything. In fact, for other organizational flaws that had emerged, the funding procedures had been halted by two of its 'curators'. Gavin Wood had already recused himself from that group before the crash, frustrated with the misperception that the term 'curator' had created with investors, he said at the time.

People tried to slow the theft down by spamming the Ethereum network, but to little avail. It only stopped once Vitalik asked the exchanges to halt trading and proposed a hard–fork (pg. 155) as solution: to effectively change the history of the blockchain that is the Ethereum mainnet.

That Vitalik publicly asked the exchanges, the exchanges stopped trading as requested and the heist stopped soon after, demonstrates how important the exchanges are for the ecosystem. And how high Vitalik's authority is in the community. All this happened within hours. And both factors are, obviously, highly centralized, off–chain backstops.

The hard-fork as nuclear option.

So Vitalik proposed to change the code of all clients to make it as if The DAO had never existed. The very thing people like to argue cannot happen with a blockchain, which makes it great for auditing etc. Obviously, this was kind of pressing a red button. Vitalik had no problem to act decisively.

It is unclear if Vitalik's announcement really stopped the thieves. Some felt they might have calculated that stealing only $50 million and leaving $100 million in the pot would create an incentive to not push the nuclear button. Suck it up and be content with the remainder. Game theory as reverse motivation forensics. Also, many people feel that there are rather few developers who could pull something like this exploit off and they all know each other. And, some don't like each other, like by default all those who invested heavily in Bitcoin, hoping for it to *"go to the moon"*. Only to see more and more miners defect to Ethereum as the better deal.

Another Hollywood-like twist to the story was that for 27 days the thieves could not spend their loot. Because they could only steal out of the smart contracts of The DAO by *cloning* those very contracts and by this, copying and activating against themselves a security measure built into The DAO that froze funds freshly coming in. This gave the core developer community 27 frantic days to find out what to do to stop the thieves and how to implement it.

Life stopped. Religious battles ensued behind the scenes as to whether do nothing about the theft − because Ethereum had not failed, just the code of The DAO had turned out to be flawed! − And had not the loud and clear proclamation of the makers of the DAO been that *code is law!* Well, that law had not been broken.

Or, if Ethereum should be acknowledged as, in the end, a community of users and that if the community had a wish to change reality it should be free to do so.

Vitalik's stance was in sync with earlier writing of his where he embraced 'Weak Subjectivity,' which basically means that using social trust – people trusting other people – to drive consensus can often make sense:

"Consensus is a social process, and human beings are fairly good at engaging in consensus on our own without any help from algorithms [...] The reason why consensus algorithms are needed is, quite simply, because humans do not have infinite computational power, and prefer to rely on software agents to maintain consensus for us." [165]

The question remains what type of meta consensus had been violated by the machines that required humans to step in. Or more precisely, on what level had a consensus–mistake become apparent that justified to stop the guarantees the machines were designed to uphold. But it doesn't change the reality that:

The ultimate arbiter for blockchains is social consensus.

The core developers had little qualms in looking at the world they created as something malleable at will. After all, they had brought it into existence and had gone through many variations of visions about what it all should become. In their mind it was never a saint timestamping machine.

---

165 https://blog.ethereum.org/2014/11/25/proof-stake-learned-love-weak-subjectivity/

Not a distributed ledger that had value only for being unchangeable.

Then a group called *white hats* – meaning benevolent hackers – started to attack The DAO to drain out and save the remaining funds in it, adding more chaos.

Vote-by-upgrade.

The actual decision for a hard–fork was made by a vote and as befitting a blockchain, the weight of one's vote was made dependent on one's hashing power. In keeping with blockchain elegance, the vote equalled the technical switch. You made your client adopt new rules or stay the same, that was it.

This in turn demonstrated the power and importance of the miners as opposed to the fund holders. How much Ether one owned did not matter. Even someone with $100,000,000 worth of Ether but no miners running would not have had any say although their holdings turned out to be affected in a substantial way.

The vote clearly favored the hard–fork: those 'new rules' changed Ethereum clients so that The DAO kind–of never happened. And everyone who could be identified got their Ether back.

It sure helped that some in the core community – though not all – had invested into The DAO. There were laconic questions what would happen when the next smart contract went bad. A hard–fork every time then someone created a bug in a smart contract? Surely not?

It's quite exciting to contemplate a development where this procedure is built into the platform. That any type vote might lead to a controlled split of the network at any-time. But then every split reduces the security of the network, or networks. And it mushrooms the complexity for people who hold funds.

Regardless, this is what Dfinity will attempt.

What is Ethereum Classic?

Because, ha! – the way the Ethereum and Bitcoin blockchains work, a client is automatically kicked out when it misbehaves.

To make the hard–fork and wish The DAO and its heist out of existence, everyone who wanted to vote for it and participate in the forking off, had to install a new client that behaved slightly different from the old clients.

Now, for all people voting for the hard–fork, their new clients simply stopped playing with the old clients, which where not following the hard–fork, at one point – precisely, at block 1,920,000.

But to the old clients it looked the reverse: the hard–forking clients looked like they were badly misbehaving all of a sudden from block 1,920,000 and for – while the hard–forkers kicked out the guys who did not want to hard–fork – the *non*–forkers likewise kicked out the *forkers* from their network. And retained a smaller but pure net-work with unchanged ground rules. In the beginning only 1% of nodes remained.

The hard–fork resulted into two Ethereum mainnets.

So the old clients just continued their thing, justified in the 'belief' that most of their peers had gone mad but that they and some remaining others where doing the only right thing.

And now there are two mainnets. With two different types of Ether. The people staying behind immediately got a boost by one of the exchanges, which started to trade their Ether, which was called Ethereum Classic (exchange symbol ETC).

ETC is the purer choice, great for the DAO thieves and for damaging Ethereum.

There were voices that argued against the hard–fork, warning that Ethereum would lose its credibility for good. One entrepreneur crinched about how all of a sudden all the promises of irreversibility turned out to be not true at all and how that sunk the basic value proposition of block-chains. Others had invested a bit too much into The DAO to have an ear for such rather philosophical points and just hoped to get their stolen money back.

Those who were unemotional in general remarked that investing into The DAO had quite obviously been a very high risk proposition and that the decision for a hard–fork to bail the speculators out was tainting Ethereum's mission.

And then there is a notion that both Ethereum and Ethereum Classic *are* Ethereum now.

Ether Classic – the cryptocurrency of those nodes, which refused the fork – is currently[166] worth only a tenth of the

---

166 Q4 2016

'real' – now hard–forked – Ether's worth (ETH). Which is now kind of the 'real' Ethereum, with the clear majority of the community behind it. But in sum, both are not worth what Ether was worth before The DAO heist, so nobody won.

Except the DAO thieves who keep their bounty in the Ethereum Classic universe. Replay-attackers had a lot of fun, too, robbing the exchanges blind without them noticing. And all in all The DAO attackers were rather successful in damaging Ethereum in the worst possible way.

Who knows, maybe ETC is yet another mind game and the real purpose of Ethereum Classic is to tempt the thieves to move their Ether, make a mistake and get caught in the real world by good-old KYC data collected at the exchanges. Ah, well.

ETC is good for Dapps.

There is an upside to Ethereum Classic in that it is cheaper than the main Ethereum, which makes some business models possible and allows for testing on a real network at a tenth of the price.

EPILOG

*"At this point
we find ourselves
confronted by a very
disquieting question:*

*"Do we really wish
to act upon our
knowledge?"*

Aldous Huxley, 1958

What is all the Hype about?

The hype is a PR effect.

I get to talk to some people. For many big companies it tends to be about a story to calm down their share holders. Outside banking, the knowledge about blockchains is more than thin.

People who talk to even more people confirm that most decision makers still have no idea at all.

That is not too surprising because CEOs don't necessarily have to understand IT tools, which is what the blockchain is. Although in the 70's you will have benefitted to understand what a relational database could enable your company to do. And from the 90's, to imagine what the web could be used for.

But many companies still just want to be seen active in the space and at this point they spend research money scatter shot, because they can't even find people to give the money to to do meaningful research. That is not strictly their fault. Clueless enthusiasts can look very convincing opposite uninterested smart people.

A few banks clearly did their homework. Others appear genuinely unconcerned and uninterested. This leads to uninformed people making choices that make no sense, and then Sarah will tell them so. At some point people will get frustrated from all the rejection and hard limits.

Which is unfortunate, because if they would man up, go to Sarah and ask, *Well, well, we need to be seen doing something with blockchain, our domain is this and that, what would make sense for us to do?* Then Sarah or one of us would happily pore over the actual challenges of that domain with them and get down to work.

But as it goes right now, some people will just be too happy to find out that , and proud to have understood something about the confusing topic at last, tell shareholders and the public their findings, relieved that everyone can move on with their lives and leave this weird planet blockchain behind.

This is already happening to some extent.

But even when the hype comes crashing down, just like the Internet did not go away after the dot com crash, blockchains are just beginning.

Blockchains might not get as big of a name as the Internet itself. They *are* – in *this* respect – more like databases, a technology used at the back, with no need for users to know any details. Databases are everywhere but their existence is sub summized under the web site they serve or the service they are used for to implement.

But blockchain is real, here to stay and there are some big players who are getting it. There are IBM, Microsoft, Deloitte who turned out in numbers at Consensus 2016 in New York. There are basically all relevant names in banking in R3 CEV's consortium.

The question will be, is Consensys the next Google or Yahoo. And how come, really, that the next Sergey Brin is again from Russia.

What's the Future?

Ethereum is the best blockchain. Today.

Ethereum has a first mover advantage in a network domain. It has momentum, traction, grabs headlines; devs love it despite all its technical short comings and immaturities; it is used on every hackathon where people have a free choice what blockchain technology to pick.

There are powerful contenders in the ring now for the crown, with infinitely deep pockets and deadly serious ambition but none of them is aiming at the exact same turf as Ethereum does:

> Ethereum is a chain for everyone, hardened for public exposure, designed for interoperability and openness first.

The competition will hopefully spur innovation with interesting contributions to the tough problems to be solved, and because most efforts are Open Source this could result into a rich ecosystem with different chains addressing different needs.

There are at least three new blockchains coming up from members of the wider Ethereum community, two under the radar at this point, and Dfinity just announced. If they have answers to hard problems, they deserve success but will have a very hard time building the same breadth of developer community and name recognition that Ethereum now has.

Specialized blockchains will not look like blockchains.

Special–purpose blockchains will, also, not *be* blockchains but will be employing, recycling and re–dressing great ideas that have come to the fore in the wake of blockchains. There is nothing wrong with *Enigma*,[167] Guardtime, BigChainDB or Corda. They are winning propositions in a field that might well see high specialization to cater to special needs of lucrative industries. But arguably, they are not strictly blockchains. And with the exception of Guardtime, they also don't claim to be.[168]

The interesting question for every new concept is, what was traded in to gain what new feature.

Ethereum has created a strong momentum though and has the advantage now of a strong community coalescing around its general purpose paradigm.

---

167 Enigma is a seminal project to create a blockchain–based cloud platform using the vaunted approach of *secure multi-party computation* to achieve data privacy – http://enigma.media.mit.edu

168 Guardtime claims to run a blockchain for you, on their servers, to create timestamps. It has naught to do with decentralization, decentralized code, smart contracts or cryptocurrencies.

The main task for everyone else is to find their niche and that traction.

The core developer community is splitting up.

That's as long announced and should give innovation a boost.

There were intense struggles about the right course throughout. The question of a commercial entity was contentious and many early members left over the years, more or less frustrated and enriched. Then it was a bit of a challenge for some of the early community to adjust when the money started poring in.

Still the core team managed to hold together until the mainnet was launched – and money started to run out at the end of 2015. The situation is under control now after some hard choices have been made and the value of Ether has appreciated massively. The Ether it kept for itself when it all started is the main source of funding the Ethereum Foundation has left now.

The smart and influential EthCore gang around Gavin Wood clearly strive to push innovation the way they find it makes most sense, not necessarily in line with the Ethereum Foundation. This will create a fork in the *protocol*, an even more serious event than a fork in the chain.

Because as mentioned, Ethereum really is a protocol. This split will be as substantial as The DAO hard–fork, potentially affecting the mainnet by draining miners and market cap from it like any other competitor. The way it always happens is by adding extensions that people like, start using and by that make new things that are incompatible with the original platform. Microsoft played in that way with Netscape and Java and called it *Freedom to Innovate*. But in C# they also created the better Java.

And such race might give incentive to find out how to best work *across* diverse chains to scale. There will be different, interoperating networks, running slightly different protocols. Maybe they will all have a stable user and developer base and people will have good reason to build bridges between worlds.

The Go client, geth, is perceived as the canonical Ethereum client since the Foundation made the decision in 2015 to have it vetted and released first and to focus its remaining funds on it. It's lead is so comfortable that Jeffrey Wilcke, the lead of the Go team, publicly calls on people to also use other client implantations to realize the security advantage to be gained from people using different clients (pg. 280).

Christian Reitwiessner, the implementor of Solidity, now leads the C++ effort, with the remaining manpower still funded by the Foundation. They work to improve its robustness, reduce its footprint and make it a valid option, especially for IoT.

The Ethereum user community strives.

It's hard to tell how many people can *really* program Solidity right now, it's probably just a few dozen with thousands looking at it and dabbling in it. The job market looks very good, learning Solidity should be a good investment right now for any programmer. People with a good grasp of the matter are desperately sought after but the total market is still small.[169]

---

169 If you are a total nerd reading this, please for once in your life ask
    for a realistic salary, people will be *happy* to give it to you and will still

Tools, start ups, ideas and events are springing up, many sponsored by banks and big brands. Microsoft is offering hosted Ethereum nodes and IBM has released an ambitious, forward looking Open Source platform for IoT, Blue Horizon, in its first incarnation based firmly on Ethereum.

Many fintech projects, most prominently the banking consortium R3 CEV, have used Ethereum for their early experiments because there was no real alternative. For IBM's main blockchain group, we looked at Ethereum first and learned about blockchain from it, before the decision was made to embark on the quest to create a better one, more useful for fintech, which lead to the Linux Foundation's Hyperledger project.

Joe Lubin's Consensys is a strong driver of practical Ethereum application and experimentation since day one, funding dozens of start ups in the space. His smarts, money and influence are firmly behind Vitalik, as they were from the beginning and Joe trusts "V" to find the way forward.

---

not expect infallibility from you. Hear me, F.?

Will Ethereum Change the World?

Probably.

Ethereum enables new things, based on decades of research.

If not Ethereum, something similar will come along to power smart contracts – that scale, are fast, confidential and reversible – and will change commerce and society at large to the degree that highways or the Internet did.

There are about 100 contenders in the market now, vying for becoming *the* blockchain. Most are just variations of Bitcoin, some fork Ethereum, usually they cater to a niche, often to finance.

Right now Ethereum is the best we have. It's quite ahead of the competition, it is evolving, its team delivers and is learning from mistakes. Ethereum looks poised to lead for some time to come.

The new matrix.

Blockchains will likely create an alternate reality that will at times supersede the actual reality in painful ways. Having *lost the key* might become a dreaded calamity and its unfair consequences the battle cry of luddites.

But parallel worlds like this exist already and grind unlucky individuals to shreds with the excuse of equal process for all. This can be improved.

Be it law, finance, secret services, they all create a mirror image of you in their files that you don't see and that can have serious repercussions for your life. There are rules, but no normal person can know them all, some are secret. if you match a pattern, it might affect your existence on many levels for ridiculous reasons.

Blockchains were invented to address that.

George Lucas says he created Star Wars to inspire people to envision the future. That's a good spirit to look at blockchains: how can the parallel worlds we *have* be made better by using the blockchain?

We're happy to write more and better code. Maybe you find the application. What does the Force tell you?

Wrapping up

How do you feel? I hope it was a fun ride. Thanks for reading. I honestly hope you got something out of it. I honestly hope you will re-read.

To wrap it up, let's go through the grey boxes again that highlighted the most important findings.

Ideally you should understand each one and, over time, get to know them by heart. Maybe take a pen and check what you got.

The page numbers in brackets will help you jump right to the boxes' context in case you want to refresh.

I'll leave you with that. Check out *www.ethereum.org* and Ethereum's twitter feed at *@ethereumproject*.

Give me a shout what you thought was stupid at *ethereum.book@gmail.com*. Credits! Follow me at *@hdiedrich* – meet me at one of the conferences!

Thx*!*

*Blockchains collapse
agreement and execution.* (3)

*Blockchains are about
guarantee of execution.* (5)

*Bitcoins are digital but
cannot be copied.* (6)

*Blockchains introduce
digital scarcity.* (7)

*Ethereum programs
cannot be stopped.* (7)

*Blockchains are like
a force of nature.* (7)

*You can't
defeat a protocol.* (8)

*Every blockchain
node is equal.* (9)

*Decentralization pre-empts
outside control.* (9)

*Blockchains enable machines to do
business directly with other machines.* (13)

*Blockchains prevent things from
going wrong in the first place.* (14)

*With blockchains, programs take
on a life of their own.* (15)

*Writes to a blockchain are
global and permanent.* (18)

*Data and programs on the
blockchain are auditable.* (19)

*Public blockchains introduce
a new type of security.* (20)

*Who doesn't agree – is simply
kicked off the network.* (21)

*Smart contracts
will execute.* *(22)

*Ethereum smart contracts
have code and memory.* (28)

*Ethereum is the
blockchain of blockchains.* (29)

*The contract
is the money.* (31)

*Ethereum is free.
No one owns it.* (32)

*Every node in a blockchain stores
and computes the same data.* (33)

*Everyone calculating everything
does not scale. Not at all.* (34)

*Because everything is signed,
there is no need to trust.* (35)

*Ethereum is the fastest platform
for decentralized applications.* (36)

*It's fast to write decentralized
applications for Ethereum.* (36)

*Having the contracts on-chain
might be the killer difference.* (38)

A Blockchain survives
as long as one node stays up. (40)

Crypto
is fiat. (45)

Ethereum is many magnitudes slower
than today's databases. (49)

Many 'blockchain' ideas should use
a database or cloud service instead. (49)

If it doesn't need guaranteed execution,
it's not a blockchain use case. (50)

Ethereum can be up to 10 magnitudes
slower than other platforms. (51)

Real products will usually
mix on- and off-chain code. (52)

Ethereum was made to
exchange the gearbox in—flight. (55)

Blockchains allow for bearer-like,
yet perfectly auditable instruments. (63)

Blockchains add
the dimension of trust to data. (78)

A blockchain protects the accounts
when a node is compromised. (79)

Blockchains might soon
not have ledgers anymore. (96)

Crypto is
trap-door math. (103)

A digital signature
uses a secret key. (103)

A digital signature
also needs a 'public key'. (105)

Bitcoin and Ethereum are
not encrypted. Yet. (105)

Hashes are the
links of Cypherspace. (108)

Two different data sets will 'always'
result into two different hashes. (109)

Keys are secret numbers
that work like cash. (112)

Total validation
replaces central control. (113)

Cryptocurrency empowers
smart contracts. (114)

Knowing its private key
means possessing the account. (115)

The key is
the authorization. (116)

Key ownership
can be repudiated. (116)

All accounts 'pre-exist.'
You just grab a random key for one. (117)

The blockhash fixes which
transactions, in what order. (119)

The nested chain of blockhashes,
is the 'chain' in 'blockchains.' (119)

*Past transactions become the harder
to revert the older they are. (120)*

*Blockchains
substitute for trust. (122)*

*Blockchains replace
intermediaries with mathematics. (123)*

*Blockchains, by design,
can lose data. (124)*

*Making nodes unreachable is a
major attack vector on blockchains. (126)*

*Anyone can see
every transaction. (128)*

*Cryptocurrency is
decentralized digital money. (133)*

*Consensus means that nodes
agree on the same world state. (142)*

*The responsibility to stay with the
majority opinion is shifted to the node. (145)*

Proof–of–work
is non–interactive. (146)

Proof–of–work incentivizes consensus
instead of enforcing it. (147)

Proof–of–stake may replace the
wasteful, centralizing proof–of–work. (152)

A hard–fork
can re–write history. (155)

Decentralized code
cannot be altered or shut down. (160)

Smart contracts
dis-intermediate the intermediaries. (172)

Smart contracts allow for new
markets by forcing honesty. (173)

Smart contracts cannot reach
information outside the blockchain. (174)

One smart contract will almost never
replace exactly one legal contract. (175)

*Smart contracts are part of
one big formula: the complete chain.* (178)

*Smart contracts live
in Cypherspace.* (179)

Decentralized code → smart contract → DAO. (181)

*Oracles feed smart contracts
information from beyond the chain.* (187)

*The EVM is the
industry standard.* (203)

*Transactions are not guaranteed to
make it into the blockchain.* (209)

*A blockchain transfer is
very fast to finality.* (217)

*An Ethereum transaction is
considered final after twelve blocks.* (218)

*Blockchains commit state
very slowly.* (219)

*Blockchains have a
very small capacity.* (221)

*As with cash, it will be impossible
to stop all unlawful activities.* (243)

*The ultimate arbiter for blockchains
is social consensus.* (290)

*Ethereum is a chain for everyone, hardened for public
exposure, designed for interoperability and openness first.*
(302)

=★=

APPENDIX

*"Much to learn,
you still have. "*

Yoda

Hello, World! Up Close

Maybe an indisputable receipt is not that impressive, out of all context. But let's dissect this script to get your toes wet.

```
contract Hello {
  event Log(bytes32 msg);
  function Hello() {
    Log("Hello, World!");
  }
}
```

The first line basically starts a class definition, with the keyword in Solidity for that not being *class* but – *contract*.

You can instantiate many contracts with this script, by deploying it multiple times, and somewhat unfortunately, all these individual deployed instances of the contract will usually also be called *contracts*.

This is because more often than not, contracts will be thought of as *singletons*[170]. Most contracts are designed to be deployed once, as one instance. But in practice, as soon as code is improved and re-deployed as a better version, you have two instances out there. You may not be interested in the old instance any more and stay with the notion that your contract script is always only deployed once and so it's all one. But it's blurry.

---

170 Something which exists only once. Using singletons is frowned upon in much of CS but it makes life easier for scripters.

And to make matters even more confusing, there are two other, significant meanings of the term *contract* in Ethereum: legal contracts and smart contracts. The former being those contracts lawyers care about and the latter a special type of script, defined by the fact that it moves money or any other digital asset.

So for the sake of clarity, let's talk about the lines in this script as a *contract class*. Obviously, this contract class is called 'Hello'.

The next line then defines something interesting, an *event*.

```
event Log(bytes32 msg);
```

The programmer's choice here was to call that event 'Log'. But no matter the name, an event, when called, always simply creates a log entry.

The line declares the contents type of the future log message. When this event declaration is later used

```
Log("Hello, World!")
```

it logs the message "Hello, World!" to the global Ethereum blockchain.

Technically, it's not *really* written into the blocks, but to its *receipt logs*, which are part of what the blockchain vouches for. Someone trying to erase all proof that you did log "Hello, World!" at that given time would have to try to alter the blockchain or bribe all its nodes. Or alter the client code, distribute it and convince people to vote for a hard–fork.

That this is difficult, is what blockchains are all about.

HelloCoin, Up Close

The code is pretty self-explanatory. It defines the contract class *HelloCoin*.

```
contract HelloCoin {
    mapping (address => uint) public balance;
    function mint(address receiver, uint amount) {
        balance[receiver] += amount;
    }
    function send(address receiver, uint amount) {
        balance[msg.sender] -= amount;
        balance[receiver] += amount;
    }
}
```

The static state that this contract keeps is a map called *balance* that maps addresses, i.e. account numbers, of anyone using Ethereum to an amount of HelloCoins that the contract instance will be guardian of.

```
mapping (address => uint) public balance;
```

'Anyone' as in, if there is no entry for you, then you don't have any.

Although we are in a decentralized world here, and this code is run thousands of times only to get the same result – blockchain-style – this is a singleton. It's essential how the

Replication across nodes is orthogonal to contract instances.

It's one instance. It's just replicated thousands of times. But that doesn't mean they all live their own lives and would have to be taken care of separately. The replicas behave as one.

Now, the function *mint* creates new HelloCoins. It simply adds a number of coins to the receiver's balance as you tell it to in a call to it.

```
function mint(address receiver, uint amount) {
    balance[receiver] += amount;
}
```

And *send* transfers them from any one Ethereum account to another. The balance is not stored *in* the accounts though but exclusively in your static *balance* map. Plain to see, it just subtracts the given amount from the sender account's map entry and adds it to the receiver's entry in the map.

```
function send(address receiver, uint amount) {
    balance[msg.sender] -= amount;
    balance[receiver] += amount;
}
```

You don't have to take care about whether the map entry exists already, Solidity does that for you.

Again: the above is the definition of a *contract class*. This class can be instantiated once, or many times over. But the latter would result into the creation of multiple currencies.

Each deployed *contract instance* will have its own unique *address* – a number – that identifies it, like a memory reference identifies an instantiated object in other languages.

Note that this is a specific example, other Ethereum scripts do completely different things.

So, drilling deeper, this currency, if you deployed this code, would really be anchored in the *address* of the contract instance – there is no notion of the name HelloCoin meaning anything anymore, on the technical level, once the contract is compiled and deployed.

However, 'm*int*' and 's*end*' are used as proper names, together with the contract instance's address, to make a call to this contract.

The mind–bending point is this:

> ## Blockchains are programmed 'in a centralized way'.

Obviously, if you do the sensible thing and just create one instance, the *balance* map of this contract's singleton instance will be the one arbiter of truth as to who has how many HelloCoins.

On the surface this is very similar to an account stored on a central mainframe computer in a bank. But again, this smart contract is executed 'decentralizedly': every node in the network is going to run this exact piece of code, with exactly the same data as input as all the others.

And therefore, this balance map is not unique state somewhere on one computer but exists on all nodes of the entire network. In reliable lockstep. But it's still a singleton.

You program something like a single threaded program. But really it's executed in parallel – or rather: symmetrically – the world over. And therefore, protected against any tampering by decentralization. While still having just one well defined list of values at any given moment. And anyone claiming that the map should read differently than everyone else is simply kicking themselves off the network and not listened to anymore (see pg. 112).

The experience is much like how programming for a multi-threaded system in the end has you writing individual, sequential chunks of code.

This is the essence of decentralized programming, it's new and very easy to lose track of. It has you operating with seemingly centralized, singleton elements. But each bit is a Hydra.

And there is no notion of 'communication between threads' because the basic premise is that all threads do exactly the same. There is nothing to talk about between them. The *concept* of threads in the common sense does not exist. You think about them all as one.

How you get all computers to check each other that everyone does the same, is what Bitcoin first solved, in a brilliant way. This is where proof–of–work and *consensus* come in (pg. 142).

So how would you get the above code deployed?

1. run an Ethereum client
2. create an Ethereum account
3. deploy the code to the network

You are actually led through 1 + 2 automatically when installing an Ethereum client, as described below.

And how would you use it?

4. upon deployment, you receive an address where your contract instance now lives
5. you can then call functions mint or send using this address
6. and everyone else you tell the address, or finds it, can call those functions, too.

The HelloCoin program is not altogether pathetic.

Many special purpose currencies like this are springing to life on Ethereum. Similar scripts will govern *digital assets* (pg. 138).

Now, in reality, at the very least you would need to make sure that not everyone can *mint* HelloCoins, but only you yourself.

To this end you want to restrict who can run the *mint* function and also prevent anyone from running a negative balance.

It would also be good to have receipts, for everyone to see, when HelloCoins change hands.

Basically, this is all you need to add:

```
contract HelloCoin {
    address public minter;
    mapping (address => uint) public balance;
    event Sent(address from, address to, uint amount);
    function HelloCoin() {
        minter = msg.sender;
    }
    function int(address receiver, uint amount) {
        if (msg.sender != minter) return;
        balance[receiver] += amount;
    }
    function send(address receiver, uint amount) {
        if (balances[msg.sender] < amount) return;
        balance[msg.sender] -= amount;
        balance[receiver] += amount;
        Sent(msg.sender, receiver, amount);
    }
}
```

Installation

Go client – geth

If you have the prerequisites like git and go:

```
$ git clone \
https://github.com/ethereum/go-ethereum.git
$ cd go-ethereum
$ make geth
$ ./build/bin/geth
```

This installs and starts the most popular Ethereum client, the Go implementation, *geth*.

Your client will start, connect to the Ethereum mainnet and start *synchronizing* with it. Then you're ready to create your own *account* – you'll get an account number and a password – and call any smart contract existing on the mainnet. You 'call' a contract in the same sense in that you would call a persisted object, or a function library.

Rust client – Parity

The Go client had its problems recently and if you are using a Mac, this installs the Rust client instead, which weathered attacks better and also performs better:

```
$ brew tap ethcore/ethcore
$ brew install parity
$ parity
```

Clients

Go – geth

"Ethereum … is written in Go."

Well, not quite. But geth is the most popular client.

http://ethereum.github.io/go-ethereum/

Rust – Parity

"fastest and most secure"

Maybe, thanks to Rust and the team's experience.

https://ethcore.io

C++ – eth

"exceptionally portable"

http://cpp-ethereum.org

https://github.com/ethereum/cpp-ethereum

Python – pyethapp

"easily hackable and extendable"

Vitalik and Heiko use it for research for *Casper*, *sharding*, *Hydrachain* and *Raiden*.

https://github.com/ethereum/pyethapp

Permissive license.

Java – ethereumj

"can be embedded in any Java project"

https://github.com/ethereum/ethereumj

Permissive license.

Haskell – strato

"The easiest way to build Ethereum apps"

Blockapps is focussed on offering Ethereum as a service. What they actually deploy on devices are Javascript proxy clients. But there is a Haskell client and a VM at:

https://github.com/blockapps/strato-p2p-client

https://github.com/blockapps/ethereum-vm

To install check out:

https://github.com/blockapps/strato

Javascript – node-ethereum

"standalone or embeddable"

http://ethereumjs.github.io

Permissive license.

Ruby – ruby-ethereum

https://github.com/cryptape/ruby-ethereum

Permissive license.

Wallets

If you are new to this, watch out.
You can lose money.

Mist

This is the official Ethereum wallet. Download the right package for your OS, unpack and start:

https://github.com/ethereum/mist/releases

MyEtherWallet

An open source, client-side Ether wallet written in Javascript and running directly in your browser:

https://www.myetherwallet.com

Jaxx

For Android take a look at:

https://jaxx.io

Icebox

Cold storage browser tool by Consensys:

https://github.com/ConsenSys/icebox

What is Money?

Money is fulfilling multiple functions. The three most important are:

1. medium of exchange

2. store of value

3. unit of account

We use it as medium of exchange when we buy something with it. Without it, we'd still be bartering all the time. To be a medium of exchange, the currency has to be accepted by a sufficiently wide array of market participants.

To be a store of value, money should simply not lose its value over time, or not too fast. During times of hyper inflation, money loses value so fast that it becomes almost useless. Because then the money you take in, e.g. for your work loses its value faster than you can go out and by food for it. So to work as a medium of exchange it must also be a store of value, at least briefly.

As a unit of account, money simple serves as a yard-stick to compare the value of disparate things. In so far as they can be priced, they become comparable as to their perceived value.

I sometimes ask the audience at conferences, "who here understands money?" Zero to one hands go up usually. Depending on whether Nick is there. Kidding.

It's relevant because we might be projecting something into Cypherspace that is not the best abstraction: the *coin*.

About the Author

At IBM, I was called our most knowledgeable guy in blockchain, while our competition graciously called me a thought leader in the field. I am now working with the European Commission to find out if blockchains can help averting liquidity crises like 2008.

As architect of the IBM Blockchain group, I wrote the first white paper for IBM's Open Blockchain, which was later contributed to the Linux Foundations' Hyperledger.

For a short while I was one of the lone standard bearers – Yoda and I – of IBM's fledgeling IoT–blockchain research, ADEPT. We got heavy internal flak. I kept getting the word out and a little later it could not be enough blockchain for IBM IoT.

I got into blockchain because I am fascinated by the technology, the same as with language design, database architecture or coding in the first place. I was sold really when I realized Bitcoin solved something I had concluded was unsolvable.

In blockchain tech, many domains coalesce that I have worked in. I started programming age 12 hacking computer games, and always remained passionate about performance and whatever resembles 'AI'. I worked in fintech, distributed databases and functional programming, domains that are all of special significance for the future of blockchain at this point. I created a compiler and virtual machine for the insurance industry, which an eternity before it, looked eerily like Bitcoin's VM. I started programming crypto stuff a decade ago.

I am evangelizer for the best distributed, high-velocity database out there, VoltDB, and suffered with them through different stabs at solving distribution. Which is what the blockchain community re-lives right now.

In a way, it's all coming together for me in blockchains. I had to fall for it.

Detailed Index

THE WORLD COMPUTER

ETHEREUM

50685713R00202

Made in the USA
San Bernardino, CA
30 June 2017